DANCE STUDIES
THE BASICS

Dance Studies: The Basics is a concise introduction to the study of dance ranging from the practical aspects such as technique and choreography to more theoretical considerations such as aesthetic appreciation and the place of dance in different cultures. This book answers questions such as:

- Exactly how do we define 'dance'?
- What kinds of people dance and what kind of training is necessary?
- How are dances made?
- What do we know about dance history?

Featuring a glossary, chronology of dance history and list of useful websites, this book is the ideal starting point for anyone interested in the study of dance.

Jo Butterworth is currently Professor of Dance Studies at the University of Malta where she established a new department in 2010. Formerly Senior Lecturer at the University of Leeds, she was also responsible for the MA in Choreography at Fontys Dansacademie, The Netherlands.

The Basics

DANCE STUDIES
THE BASICS

Jo Butterworth

Routledge
Taylor & Francis Group

LONDON AND NEW YORK

First published 2012
by Routledge
2 Park Square, Milton Park, Abingdon, Oxon OX14 4RN

Simultaneously published in the USA and Canada
by Routledge
711 Third Avenue, New York, NY 10017

Routledge is an imprint of the Taylor & Francis Group, an informa business

British Library Cataloguing in Publication Data
A catalogue record for this book is available from the British Library

Library of Congress Cataloging in Publication Data
Butterworth, Jo.
  Dance studies: the basics/Jo Butterworth.
  p. cm. – (The basics)
  Includes bibliographical references and index.
  1. Dance. 2. Choreography. 3. Dance–History. I. Title.
  GV1594.B88 2012
  792.7'8–dc23

                                                              2011020909

ISBN: 978-0-415-58254-4 (hbk)
ISBN: 978-0-415-58255-1 (pbk)
ISBN: 978-0-203-15699-5 (ebk)

Typeset in Bembo
by Wearset Ltd, Boldon, Tyne and Wear

MIX
Paper from
responsible sources
FSC® C004839

Printed and bound in Great Britain by
TJ International Ltd, Padstow, Cornwall

CONTENTS

ACKNOWLEDGEMENTS

'Nutcracker, Interrupted: Mark Morris The Hard Nut Is a Delightfully Zany Take on the Beloved Holiday Ballet' by Curtis Wong – Content Copyright 2011 Huffington Post.com, used with permission. Roy, Sanjoy (2010) 'Celebrating Trisha Brown', first published in the *New Statesman* on 29 November 2010, used with permission.

Many people have influenced the writing of this book. Thanks to all the students whom I have been lucky enough to encounter, and to the teaching staff with whom I have shared the journey: my dear dance colleagues at Bretton Hall, University of Leeds (Chris Lomas, Evelyn Jamieson, Janet Smith, Jackie Smith-Autard, Sita Popat, Vicky Hunter, Rita Marcalo, Diane Harold and Brigitte Moody), at Fontys Dansacademie in Tilburg (Jacques van Meel, Paul de Greef, Caroline Ribbers, Dirk Dumon, Heike Salzer and Lorna Sanders) and in my new endeavour at the University of Malta (Mavin Khoo, Doris Zarb, Francesca Tranter, Rebecca Carmilleri, Heike and Lorna again). Grateful thanks to Mavin for intelligent conversations and inspiration, Sandra Mifsud for support, suggestions, formatting and glossary, and to various friends who have answered email queries across the globe.

INTRODUCTION

If we define dance as 'movement in time and space', then the first thing to say is that everyone can dance. Everyone has a personal and expressive way of moving the body; it's the first level of communication, before speech. Next, a high percentage of us get involved with dance in our lives, either doing it, participating in it, making it, teaching it or watching it as spectators. We enjoy dance's physicality, its feeling, its social interaction or its aesthetic. We may have different motives, expectations and desires, but dance gives us pleasure. Third, and this might come as quite a surprise, students and scholars all over the world are learning or teaching Dance Studies as a discipline in the university. In faculties of Performance, or Education, Arts or Technology, Dance is a growth area of study at both undergraduate and postgraduate levels. This book is specifically about the fundamentals of Dance Studies, to introduce intending students, their parents and careers teachers to what is usually studied in the first year or two.

Today, in Europe, America, Africa, Australasia and the Asia-Pacific region, students can enter university to study Dance. These courses will no doubt acknowledge their own geographical, historical and cultural dimensions, their country's demographic, but the core subjects of the discipline will be retained: the training of dance performance skills, compositional methods, practices and applications, dance history and contextual studies, dance pedagogy and dance technology.

But a word of warning: studying Dance in the university sector is not a soft option. Not only do students need to be able to dance to a reasonable level before they enter a Dance Studies programme;

understanding and studying Dance from the perspective of philosophy, aesthetics or cultural studies demands intellectual stamina and requires more than a desire to perform.

Do you think you can dance? Consider how many youngsters take part in dance classes every week. You might have done it yourself, when you were younger, perhaps been a cheer leader or taken some ballet or tap exams and still have the certificates to prove it. You may enjoy clubbing at the weekend, or attend music festivals in the summer, shaking your body and stamping your feet to rock, pop, blues, reggae, folk or bluegrass. Is hip hop and b-boying your thing? Or you may be one of the millions of television viewers who are hooked on *Strictly Come Dancing*, the UK's favourite ballroom dance television programme, *Dancing with the Stars* (USA) or *So You Think You Can Dance* in Australia, Canada or the United States. Such a broad spectrum of different kinds of dancing – to perform as art or cultural belief, to perpetuate a tradition, to watch, to join in, to socialize with friends, to get fit, to chill out ... And with the appropriate kinds of analytical skills, these forms can all be researched, investigated and interrogated.

Like many other human experiences, dance today is affected by globalization. Through travel, migration or cheap air flights, we cross borders and experience new ways of moving or other people's established traditions. Technology seems to have made the world smaller and communication more accessible, challenging our assumptions and offering us alternative views of the world and our own part in it. We can marvel at the cultural dance forms of other countries, and create new forms of dance expression by learning, sharing and borrowing.

This range of dance activities can be 'mapped' to identify professional or amateur forms; it is found in theatrical, educational or social applications; dance can utilize highly technical dance language or use ordinary, everyday pedestrian movement; it can involve a group or be an individual endeavour. For example, depending on where you live, you can see local groups of Irish dancers in Dublin, Boston or New South Wales, learn country dancing or creative dancing in school, watch urban dance on MTV and attend a ballet class in every city in the world. Do you enjoy musicals like *The Sound of Music*, *West Side Story*, *Hairspray*, or *Billy Elliot*, or films like *Black Swan*? Perhaps you have danced round the kitchen to old musical films on television like those starring Ginger Rogers and Fred Astaire or Gene Kelly in some of their amazing dance routines? Or had the opportunity to learn flamenco dance or Argentine tango?

Do you think you can dance? And, more to the point, have you ever considered studying Dance full time at university? Although more and more students want to study the subject, the vast majority of their teachers and parents have no idea what 'studying Dance' might entail. What will you *do*, they ask, and why? Wouldn't you prefer to study medicine, law or teaching?

So here is the first bit of information, the counter-argument. Everything in Dance Studies is studied both in theory and in practice, as students are expected to be able to fully understand what they learn in the dance studio, to document, analyse and reflect upon it. When they take part in a dance technique class, they need to apply both somatic and anatomical knowledge in developing their skills; when creating new dance works (choreographies) they need to demonstrate craft of choreography and their understanding of creative processes. In order to write essays, just as in any other discipline, they learn to research, collect data from books and articles, decide upon a theoretical framework, analyse, evaluate and construct an argument. Many people are sceptical about the place and treatment of dance in the university sector, but my experience of teaching Dance Studies at undergraduate and postgraduate levels in three different countries leads me to believe that intelligent and talented young choreographer-practitioners are hungry to learn beyond the boundaries of their discipline; they are naturally curious, creative individuals, excellent problem-solvers, who enjoy being introduced to new ideas from semiotics, phenomenology, cultural studies, gender studies, aesthetics and other disciplines; they gain great confidence from developing the ability to argue their case in essays, presentations and dissertations, and often find that literature new to them can be inspirational to their creative processes in making new dance work. Artistry feeds scholarship, and vice versa. Experiencing dance means *doing* and *thinking* in an integrated way.

Can you see yourself as a multi-skilled individual who can choreograph, teach, perform, and also write and present your research about dance? Would you like to be commissioned to work within the community, or to work with actors or musicians, to facilitate dance in education or in therapeutic contexts, to research, be a dance critic, direct ballets, contemporary dance or musicals, or make dancefilms for television? Reading this book might be the first step on the ladder towards a future career in dance.

A glossary of dance terms is provided on p. 191.

1

TRAINING FOR DANCE

Today, in the twenty-first century, there is a great sense of inter-disciplinarity and hybridity about the ways in which young people begin the process of preparation for studying Dance at university or college or commencing professional dance training. Through extensive travel and the internet, so much is being shared globally. Of course, in almost every country of the world, schools and academies offer professional training in chosen genres and styles, for those who have the talent, the physical acumen and the mental and creative capacity to join a company and dance professionally. Ballet and jazz dance are taught in almost every country of the world; one can learn modern dance Graham technique in Java, Chinese and South Asian dance in the UK or Singapore, Egyptian belly dancing in the USA or Australia, tango and flamenco in Israel and indeed in most countries of the world.

For those who choose to enter the dance profession as intending professional performers, either in the East or the West, the normal training period is generally understood to be at least 10 years. Young people might start with one class a week, but serious training means all day everyday classes and rehearsals in a variety of styles; in order to prepare the body for daily rehearsal or performance, in whatever genre, exercises progress from the simple to the complex, in terms of coordination, length and difficulty. Most professional students attend specialist ballet school for more than five years and/or follow an intensive three- or four-year programme at 16+.

For amateur groups learning traditional and country dance forms, like Irish clogging or Appalachian step dancing, groups might meet once or twice a week, but for those involved with competitions and regular performances, such as ballroom and Latin American dance, much more regular practice is the norm. Some forms are learned in the social or cultural context of the family or community, such as many traditional African, Aboriginal or Native American dances, while others need specialist teachers or gurus as in the South Asian styles of Bharata Natyam or Kathak.

In the higher education sector (18+), which is the specific focus of this book, students may not become professional dancers, but they may wish to make a career in dance through teaching, performing, choreographing, running creative workshops or open classes or managing dance events. Therefore, they need to be able to dance, to the best of their ability; during the three or four years of study, they will probably be introduced to several different forms of technique.

The majority of dance students who enter college or university to study dance have been introduced to dancing by attending private ballet or dance schools. All over the world these schools offer classes based on syllabus work and examinations in classical ballet and other forms. Dance teaching societies which offer training for teachers and examination syllabi for their students include: the British Ballet Organization (BBO), the American Association of Ballet (AAB), the Royal Academy of Dance (RAD) and the Cecchetti Society – the Cecchetti method of ballet is a style of classical, theatrical dance based on the teachings of the Italian ballet master Enrico Cecchetti (1850–1928).

- The RAD in London has 13,000 members worldwide in 79 countries run by 179 staff and 200 examiners; approximately 250,000 children and students take graded examinations each year.
- The Imperial Society of Teachers of Dancing (ISTD) offers examinations in ballet (Cecchetti and imperial), but also in a wide range of genres and styles including modern ballroom, Latin American, and the South Asian dance styles of Bharata Natyam and Kathak.
- The International Dance Teachers Association (IDTA) claims 7,000 members in 55 countries.
- NZAMD (New Zealand Association of Modern Dance) was the first New Zealand-based dance examination organization, and is now one of the largest in the country with over 270 teacher members and nearly 14,000 students involved in examinations.

These and other organizations offer syllabus training followed by examinations taught in private dance studios in many genres: e.g. different styles of ballet, jazz, modern and ballroom. Other students come to study dance through the dance education route, in those countries where dance is established as part of state education. This might mean that intending students have been following dance in a National Curriculum, in contemporary/modern style, South Asian, ballet or African contemporary, for example, in GCSE or A level.

In order to study Dance in the university or college, the normal entry qualification is the required matriculation of the country, plus an audition designed to test dance technical skills, choreographic or performance experience, anatomical/skeletal fitness and the ability to communicate verbally about aspects of the wider dance field. Some institutions wish to see intending students respond to improvisation tasks or small group activity.

For many years there have been clear distinctions between professional and educational dance institutions in relation to their approaches to teaching and learning. In a balletic context, the goal in training a dancer usually relates to getting into a company. In professional dance contexts, including vocational dance training, dancers are trained through daily immersion in technique classes, in rehearsals with choreographers or répétiteurs (where the concern is with the making of new works or with the reconstruction of existing choreography) and through the regular performance of completed works. Formerly, dancers tended to become choreographers through the apprentice method, drawing upon their personal experiences as dancers in relation to the 'master' choreographers. Today, however, many curricula in university-validated degree programmes include choreography. Students practise technique, but also study choreography and improvisation, engaging with the creative process and the development of understanding and application of the methods, concepts and principles of dance and choreography. The old perception among professional vocational teachers, that it is difficult to fuse notions of curiosity, creative exploration and critical faculty with rigorous technical training, has finally been laid to rest. Leaving aside the objectives of each institute/programme, and the personal desires of each student, today a balanced approach is advocated, where the principles of technical mastery, critical faculty and creativity can be pulled into correspondence and students have the opportunity to make, perform or study Dance wherever they apply and are offered a place.

The next section of this chapter investigates training rituals and objectives. First, three examples have been chosen from non-Western locations – Beijing in China, Ghana in Africa and Tamil Nadu in India – to demonstrate the structures and context of the education of young dancers. We then consider the specific training activities of ballet, modern/contemporary and somatic techniques that have been predominant in the West. However, it will soon become evident that the traditional dichotomies between one part of the world and another have become less relevant under the influences of travel, globalization and technology.

EXEMPLAR 1: DANCE EDUCATION IN BEIJING, CHINA

The Chinese people believe the air is most densely charged with vital energy called *chi* at daybreak, and for thousands the day starts with dawn exercises in parks. Individuals or groups gather to jog, dance, practise the gentle slow motion of tai chi chuan or the vigorous gymnastics of kung fu. Many forms of dance training in China can be traced back thousands of years, yet after the founding of the People's Republic of China, proper dance education and research began with the establishment of the Beijing Dance Academy, which allowed dance training to be standardized. While discovering and preserving the particular style of Chinese classical dance movements, the Academy also constantly improved on its techniques in order to standardize the form, such as: foundation techniques of Chinese classical dance (barre work training, centre work training, and training jumps, turns, somersaults and combined technique), Chinese classical dance posture and rhythm training, tanzigong training (fighting and acrobatics/martial arts), sword-dance training, long-sleeve dance training, etc.

The Beijing Dance Academy, also known as the Beijing Dance Institute, is the only institution of higher education in Dance in mainland China. There are three specialties: Performance, Choreography and Dance Studies. It offers Master's degrees and Bachelor's degrees. The school was founded on 6 September 1954 and is located in Haidian District, Beijing. There are almost 500 teachers and administrative staff and about 2,000 students. Admission to the school is competitive; an examination is required, as for all other academies. The Beijing Dance Academy also teaches pre-kindergarten, elementary, middle and high school students. Students attend full-time school at the academy and learn basic mathematics, reading, writing and other standard subjects. Students also choose a specialism such as ballet or Chinese traditional dance.

Broadly speaking, in terms of the development of Chinese modern and contemporary dance, it seems that all forms of dance, both with and without specific national characteristics and classical patterns, could be included in Chinese modern dance. Note that Chinese modern dance pioneers like Wu Xiaobang, Dai Ailian and Jia Zuoguang had intensive professional training in Western modern dance. In their dancing, they retain the spirit of freedom and innovation, while pursuing the national character of China and the trends of the time, and combine these with what they were taught. The dance classics of the Chinese modern dance of the twentieth century are represented by great works such as *March of the Volunteers* (first performed in 1934) and *Song of the Guerrillas* (1937 – during the Second Sino-Japanese War).

At the beginning of the 1960s, Wu Xiaobang set up the Tianma Dance Art Studio to promote his own teaching system which originated from modern dance. His works of this period include the *Great Ambuscade*, *Three Variations of Plum Blossom* and *Wild Geese Landing on the Sand*, which all sustain a traditional cultural spirit. Some dances were based on modern life, like *Soccer Dance* and *Butterfly*. Chinese modern dance began a new development trend at the beginning of the 1980s with the deepening of China's reforms. In recent years China directly brought in 'authentic' Western modern dance and started new explorations into this field. Guangzhou, the pioneer of Chinese reform, and Beijing, the political capital and cultural centre, became the bases for modern dance. In 1987, the first experimental modern dance class opened in Guangdong Province; in 1991, the Beijing Dance Institute officially launched the Modern Dance Teaching and Research Office. Many well-known Western modern dance experts were invited to China to give systematic training in shape and choreography, including Sarah Stackhouse, Ruby Shang, Douglas Nielson, Claudia Gittleman, Lucas Hoving, Birgit Akesson, Ren Lu Wang and Chang Ching from the United States, Britain, Sweden, Canada and Australia.

Soon after, young Chinese modern dancers began to emerge on the world stage with their unique style. The pioneers were Qin Liming and Qiao Yang from the Guangdong modern dance class, who gained the gold medal for the pas de deux at the fourth Paris International Modern Dance Contest in 1990 with the dances *Passing Voice* (choreographed by Cao Chengyuan) and *Impression of Taiji*. Later, in 1994 and 1996, gold medals at the sixth and seventh Paris International Modern Dance Contests were won by Chinese Xing Liang and Sang Jijia. Today, Chinese artists of international standard have joined major ballet and contemporary companies globally.

EXEMPLAR 2: DANCE EDUCATION IN GHANA

In the early 1960s, President Kwame Nkrumah of Ghana initiated a National Theatre Movement to help bridge the existing gap between the acquisition of theoretical knowledge and performance ability in the arts (and between African and Western artistic values) and so create viable artistic products of music, dance and drama. The Institute of African Studies at the University of Ghana took responsibility for studying the arts of Africa: a School of Music, Dance and Drama and a National Dance Company operated for the purposes of teaching, research and performance. Students from other African countries came to study and to share their knowledge of African music, dance and drama and related subjects. Traditional dancers and musicians from all over the country were recruited and integrated to form the nucleus of the National Dance Company.

As a result, three phases of dance development – *neo-traditional*, *dance-theatre*, and *contemporary dance* – emerged in Ghana alongside traditional forms. Albert Mawere Opoku pioneered the neo-traditional phase, bringing together existing traditional dances from around the country, and carefully rearranged their movements to suit the conventional stage. In phase two, a distinct Ghanaian dance-theatre began to emerge. The use of modern production methods did much to bring the many elements into a coherent unity of expression of various themes. The first serious dance-theatre production in Ghana was Opoku's *African Liberation Dance*

Suite (1965). It was followed by productions including Nii-Yartey's *The Lost Warrior* (1978) and *The King's Dilemma* (1979); *The Maidens* (1992) by Patience Kwakwa; *The Orphan* (1996) and *The Palm Wine Drinkard* (2002) by Ofotsu Adinku; and *Odwira* (2001) by Asare Newman. Since African dance is integrative – that is, it combines dance with music, drama, poetry and costumes for its expression – these choreographers used adventurous and provocative movements, with the other artistic elements, to help maintain the traditional marriage between dance and these art forms.

The third phase of contemporary African dance is now emerging. Its language, inspiration, content and symbols are drawn from the African experience. However, to advance African dance *beyond* the old form, and for its appeal to transcend its original community context, other acceptable methods and techniques of dance composition, developed from within and outside Africa, are required to achieve a viable and credible contemporary choreographic creation in Africa. Essentially, contemporary African dance must synthesize old dance traditions with innovation, technical skill and originality in evolving its own choreographic language.

Contemporary African dance is being developed by choreographers who have acquired a holistic outlook that informs their teaching and their choreographic and technical methods. Pioneers who are helping to change the face of African dance through their writings, teaching, choreographic works and performances in their respective countries and beyond include Germaine Acogny of Senegal, Alphonse Tierou and Adiatu Massidi of Côte d'Ivoire, Elsa Wolliaton of Kenya, Achille Ngoye of the Congo, Nii-Yartey of Ghana, Peter Badejo of Nigeria and Kariamu Welsh of the USA.

At the forefront of the development of contemporary African dance in Ghana is the Noyam African Dance Institute. Noyam, which translates as 'development' or 'moving on', was set up in 1998 to provide opportunity for diverse groups of young people with differing educational backgrounds to access knowledge of dance and to help advance the development of contemporary African dance in Ghana. This includes the development of a specific 'Noyam' technique derived from the movement characteristics, aesthetic qualities and philosophy of the African dance traditions. In order to acquire the movement skills needed for the effective execution and definition of this form of dance, students are taken through a selection of traditional dance movements, ensuring that they learn the proper execution and details of each dance, paying particular attention to shape, dynamics and the contextual and emotional qualities of the movements. Kinetic energy derived from such everyday human activities as falling, lifting, jumping, walking, clapping, rolling, pushing and pulling, running, the natural undulation of the spine and facial expressions of all sorts are employed in the process of building the vocabulary. Movement phrases are applied in their original form or abstracted, extended, stylized and filtered towards the creation of choreographic works in the Institute (Nii-Yartey, 2009).

EXEMPLAR 3: SOUTH ASIAN DANCE FORMS IN TAMIL NADU

South Asian dance encompasses forms originating in the Indian sub-continent and those developing in the diaspora. The subcontinent has given birth to varied forms of dancing, each shaped by the influences of a particular period and region or environment. Indian dance is, like other forms, an extremely intricate art requiring skill, hard work and discipline. All Indian dances tend to portray some expression of life and either the dance posture (Nritya) has a specific meaning or they are purely aesthetic (Nritta). Dance themes are derived from mythology, folklore, legends and classical literature.

Indian dance is said to have originated from the *Natya Shastra*, a detailed script on aspects of Indian dance written by Bharata Muni in the second century BC. The two main divisions of dance are classical and folk forms. There are dance forms typical of certain parts of the country and these are based on ancient dance discipline. The various classical forms are Bharata Natyam of Tamil Nadu, Kuchipudi of Andhra Pradesh, Odissi of Orissa, Kathak from Jaipur and Lucknow, Kathakali from Kerala and Manipuri from Manipur. The unique feature of Indian classical dances is that they are all devotional in content. Some believe that Bharata Natyam is the oldest and the purest Indian classical dance.

In India, traditional dance teaching–learning activity has tended to take place in the *gurukula* system, the indigenous system of imparting knowledge through the rigorous training of the pupil by a guru, where pupils stay in the home of the guru to master the art form in a teacher-centric way.

The history of the Bharata Natyam dance form is inextricably linked with social and political factors, in that colonialism seems to have had a negative effect (see, for example, the attempt to abolish dance in Hindu temples, assuming that *devadasis* – temple dancers – were also courtesans). Colonialists justified imperial rule by claiming that reform would 'civilize' government and economy, bringing European values. However, according to O'Shea (2007), the revival of the form hinged upon the dance's intersection with nationalism and regionalism which led to a strong revival and reconstruction of the form, to embrace diverse understandings of both traditional and more creative individual approaches. From within the region, solo dance performers of the 1920s and 1930s brought South Indian dance to the modern urban concert stage, as a stage art. Rukmini Devi was one of those dancers who helped to accelerate the revival.

Kalakshetra is a cultural academy dedicated to the preservation of traditional values in Indian art, especially in the field of Bharata Natyam dance and Gandharvaveda music. The academy was founded in January 1936 by Rukmini Devi Arundale in Tamil Nadu. Under Arundale's guidance the institution achieved national and international recognition for its unique style and perfection. In 1962, Kalakshetra moved to a new campus in Besant Nagar, Chennai, India. The Kalakshetra website explains:

> Kalakshetra Foundation is an institution dedicated to the teaching of the arts in a traditional gurukul setting. Since it was established in the early part of the twentieth century, the College has had venerated gurus in music and dance on its faculty, and they have shaped the way in which the arts are taught here. Students live and study in simple surroundings closely connected to nature. Open spaces, spreading trees, buildings which are open to the light and the breeze, cultivate a spirit of reverence for learning and for the environment. India's most respected performers are among its many alumni. Most of the faculty at the institute today were themselves students of Kalakshetra and they cherish the ideals they learnt from their gurus, passing them on,

in turn, to the students who come here to learn the traditional arts of Bharata Natyam and Carnatic Music. Kalakshetra offers Diploma courses in dance, music, instruments and fine arts and Post Diploma study in music and dance. The Director of Kalakshetra, Leela Samson, was herself a student of Rukmini Devi, and continues to be a performer and a teacher of the style she inherited from her guru. Leela Samson and her staff see themselves as links in a living chain which connects them to their gurus and to the founder of the institute. They are committed to preserving and sharing the values they absorbed and the purity and beauty of the dance and music style which has been central to their lives.

My colleague Mavin Khoo (a dancer/choreographer originally from Malaysia, and now lecturing in the Dance Studies division of the University of Malta) studied as a young boy with a guru in Chennai (Madras):

My training was/is under Guru Adyar K. Lakshman (Chennai) who was a direct disciple of Rukmini Devi Arundale. I was in a sense 'chosen' to embark on a learning process that really challenged the perception of time and result. I have been with my guru now for over 25 years! The length of class time was never determined. It could be 30 minutes, or it could last for up to six hours straight. It could be in the morning, afternoon or even in the middle of the night. I constantly had to be ready to 'go' seven days a week. As I stayed with my guru much of my learning was through listening and immersing myself totally within a 'life' that was without compromise. Fees were paid through performing chores around the house. Part of my training was determined by being constantly pushed to emotional and physical limits. Equal training was given in technique, music, vocal percussion, rhythm analysis, languages, *abhinaya* (genre of text communication) and classical literature. I was constantly reminded that my commitment to dance was a sacred marriage, that it would be a lifelong process of discovery and therefore no sense of merit achievement should be acquired.

I started performing at the age of 10 but graduated to become a soloist at the age of 16. To be a soloist within the Bharata

Natyam tradition is to develop a repertory of works that require solo performances that last from two to three hours at a time. It is unfortunate that, although the ratio of male dancers in Bharata Natyam is considerably high, few choose to become soloists. Many opt to develop male/female duet acts or work within ensemble choreography. This is possibly due to the fact that there are hundreds of dancers in Tamil Nadu and no government funding.

Khoo continued his education in ballet and contemporary dance in London and New York and has performed with various professional companies, but he also maintains his Bharata Natyam solo career and still has a strong relationship with his guru. He was invited to perform at Kalakshetra in February 2011.

Today, there are other possibilities for training, in cities as far afield as Manchester, Birmingham, Toronto or New York, in many South Asian forms introduced by immigrants who relocated to North America or Europe in the 1970s. These dances transcend national and cultural boundaries, and performers may be second- or third-generation South Asian Americans or Europeans. These dance forms are often practised by amateurs who wish to maintain links with the culture of their heritage or establish their social identity. As with other dance forms, some choose to learn and perform the traditional dances unchanged, while others approach them in a more innovative way, as a source for the creation of new, contemporary work.

EDUCATION AND TRAINING IN WESTERN FORMS: BALLET AND MODERN/ CONTEMPORARY

Dance education and training in the West has also tended to follow an 'apprentice' scheme model for the learning of dance technique, where the teacher is considered the authority, the expert, mentor and guide, and the learner is the instrument and interpreter of the material being taught, imitating and replicating the exercises and sequences to the best of his/her ability. Students today still follow this approach, receiving and processing instruction, trying out the exercises, receiving correction, repeating the exercise, developing the skill, etc. The teacher/instructor demonstrates and explains a particular exercise; the class absorb the information, try it out, clarify the timing and then perform the exercise; the instructor observes, corrects individuals, clarifies anatomical or stylistic information, perhaps provides some imagery to help the student experience, and repeats the exercise. Step by step, through repetition, students improve, classes become more complex, bodies gain experience, better alignment, flexibility, strength and movement memory. Through the synthesis of regular practice with a good teacher and intellectual understanding of the anatomical movement of the body in time and space, dancers develop their skills.

Dance technique classes vary from one to two hours, depending on the level of expertise. The length of training (up to 10 years) is usually related to the demands of the dance style, which require the body to extend its normal range of movement, for example the turnout and full leg extensions in ballet. Developing the mastery to do athletic feats such as complex elevations or continuous turning (called pirouettes or fouettés in ballet) can take many years. In addition, dancers develop phenomenal movement memory so as to be able to remember long sequences of dance and coordinate several movements at the same time; students in training need to develop awareness of alignment, control, flexibility and stamina, and to understand how to take care of their own instruments, their bodies. Professional dance preparation, whatever the style, makes specific anatomical and physical demands, but also requires artistic qualities such as musicality, expression and distinct communicative abilities. In addition, though contemporary dance styles tend to be more flexible as regards technical virtuosity, they often rely more heavily on the individuality and creativity of a dancer.

The dance environment for ballet, modern and contemporary techniques is usually a purpose-built or modified studio space of at least 12 by 12 metres, with a sprung floor, barres around the walls at waist height, and mirrors along one wall to allow the dancers to check their alignment in class, and also to be able to clearly follow the demonstration of the teacher. If the studio is utilized for contemporary dance then a dance floor (such as Harlequin manufactures) is normally necessary. A piano and experienced pianist or percussionist and sound system are also required.

Dancers in full-time vocational training also study related subjects such as basic applied anatomy, physiology and biomechanics, injury prevention and management, fitness, strength and somatic training for dancers, nutrition and psychology of performance. The body of a dancer is a finely tuned working tool which needs an intelligent, sensitive and disciplined approach to improve its capability and potential. Knowledge, awareness and the application of safe dance practice leads to individual responsibility and the prevention of injuries. Once dancers have gained a basic understanding of kinesiology and personal awareness of their strengths and weaknesses, they can begin to understand the common causes of injuries. No human body is perfect; within a group of dance students in training, each will be concerned with particular issues such as limited turnout, curvature of the spine or over-developed quadriceps muscles. It is important that these problems are identified early on in the programme by a tutor or physiotherapist. Self-care should include knowledge of a range of personal preventive or conditioning exercises, as well as understanding the need for sufficient rest, adequate nutrition and a healthy body weight. Over-tiredness or bad eating habits can lead to problems that may escalate; dancers tend to feel pressure to be thin, but college or university courses do not necessarily offer study units in nutrition. This issue will be discussed more fully towards the end of the chapter.

Students in training normally need to acquire a broad range of dance techniques, though not necessarily all at the same level of competency. After absorbing the general kinaesthetic principles of alignment, the student studies bodily coordination from a number of perspectives: some styles work with a sense of congruence where all the bits of the body work as one, as in classical ballet or Graham technique; other styles tend to use isolation, particular body part articulation or fragmentation, as in jazz dance technique. The movement might originate from the spine, the solar plexus or the pelvis; the body might be asked to achieve three or four different movements at the same time, depending on the genre or style. The next section will discuss some of the dance techniques which are normally included in a Dance Studies degree.

CLASSICAL BALLET

Ballet training for many starts at the age of 5 or 6 years old, and continue for at least 10 years or until the student (if he/she chooses) enters full-time training. Classes usually start at the barre, with a series of well-ordered exercises to prepare the back, legs and feet systematically to achieve alignment, develop turnout, flexibility, coordination and strength. Using the five positions of the upper and lower body, this part of the class normally includes a variety of pliés, tendus, développés, ronde de jambes, attitudes, battements and grands battements (note the French names for the steps, which can be traced back to the Academie Royale de la Danse, established in France by a group of dancing masters with special permission from Louis XIV).

The second section of the ballet class starts in the centre of the studio, where the student now concentrates on the parts of the technique concerned with épaulement (the angle of the shoulders), balancing and turning. Here we practise maintaining balance on the standing leg while the gesturing leg extends to front, side or back, with coordinated arms and long spine, and spiralling action in the shoulder girdle that allows the student to develop a good sense of alignment and presentation. Various kinds of turns and their preparation are also practised, such as pirouettes and fouettés.

The third section of the class comprises longer sequences (called enchaînements) which travel in space, often across the diagonal, and incorporate more complex coordinations, turning and elevation, and beatings of the legs (batterie) and finally, when the dancer is fully warmed up, large jumps (grands jetés) in combination with other steps and a variety of directions and transitions. This part of the class challenges coordination, elevation and stamina, but also expression, musicality, stylistic accuracy and presentation. Traditionally, at the end of the ballet class the dancers perform a *révérence* to the teacher as an acknowledgement of his/her expertise.

Because classical ballet techniques were codified by schools and academies, the form of the class does not change radically. There may be differences in style and performance quality, but it is possible for a professional dancer who travels to attend a ballet class in most cities of the world these days. And although these basic structures of the ballet class continue, companies and schools evolve their styles dependent on such aspects as traditional style (be it French, Russian Imperial, American) or socio-cultural context (training in Cuba, China or London). Training may be culturally specific, but the content and structure of the class also change depending on its purpose; for example, the participants may be doing a class in order to prepare for an RAD Grade 4 examination or in preparation to work with the stylistic and technical demands of a particular choreographer.

In a Dance Studies degree course, students may very well be offered regular ballet classes, though not necessarily for the purpose of performing professionally. Here, the function of the class may be to ensure some knowledge of the genre; to introduce specific styles; to underpin contemporary techniques; to strengthen the body and to develop control, particularly in the legs and feet; or to challenge coordination or stamina. However, the general intention will also be to help the student develop understanding of this genre, satisfy his curiosity and at the same time extend his or her technical ability and individual identity in whatever career is chosen.

MODERN/CONTEMPORARY

The forms of modern/contemporary technique training normally included in degree programmes on all five continents tend to derive from early modern dance in the USA, European modern dance or *Tanztheater* from Europe, contemporary dance of various individual practitioners, or the somatic techniques (release-based, Feldenkrais, Pilates, etc.). Many of these dance techniques were initiated by individual dancers/choreographers who used them to train themselves and their own dancers in a style appropriate for the specific needs of their own choreography (see examples in Chapter 3 on Dance theatre history). Latterly, however, the codified techniques of Graham, Humphrey, Horton and Cunningham have been passed down, adopted, amended and generally modified as individual teachers develop these forms in their own teaching context. Exercises have become simplified or made more complex; the original intention might be modified in relation to the needs of dancers in training or the individual tendencies of the teacher. Dance science has also progressed radically, due in no small measure to the International Association for Dance Medicine and Science (IADMS) and its regular annual conferences which are held in different continents, and the ensuing interest in postgraduate degrees in related subjects.

Since the assessment of these contemporary techniques is not specifically reliant on a set syllabus, there has been a great deal of development and evolution. Take, for example, the way in which the Martha Graham technique evolved in Britain under Robert Cohan in the early 1970s.

Cohan, who had danced with the Martha Graham Company from 1946 to 1957 and again from 1962 to 1969, became Artistic Director of the London School of Contemporary Dance (LCSD) in 1967. Initially the School aimed to train dancers in a pure modern dance Graham-derived technique, in order to develop 'a native style appropriate to the bodies and outlook of British people' (Howard, 1966). A series on the vocational dance schools published in *Dance and Dancers* demonstrated that the LSCD curriculum in 1969 comprised at least eight Graham classes per week, at least four classical ballet classes, a short intensive course in Laban's creative movement, dance composition, history of dance, music and art (Turnbull, 1969: 50). In some ways the insertion of this choreographer-specific technique into the UK was very challenging, and certainly became influential, but ultimately it could not support the development of new choreographic ideas until it was allowed to adapt and change.

Rarely, today, does a choreographer want to work specifically in the style of one of the modern dance 'greats'. Generally, Modern dance draws on one or more of four technical styles: Graham, Humphrey–Limón, Cunningham and release-based technique, as can be seen on the websites of many schools and academies worldwide.

For example, the Scottish Arts Council writes:

> Technique in Contemporary Dance is seen more as a tool for the dancer and a means by which to strengthen the body, increase flexibility, and through a deliberate exposure of the contemporary dancer to a wide range of techniques, to ensure versatility. Contemporary dance as a field is more concerned with examining the choreographic and performing process. The most commonly used techniques are:
>
> • Cunningham (named after the choreographer Merce Cunningham) focuses on the architecture of the body in space, rhythm and articulation. Cunningham uses the idea

of the body's own 'line of energy' to promote easy, natural movement.

- Graham (named after Martha Graham) focuses on the use of contraction, release, fall and recovery. Graham's technique is characterized by floor work and the use of abdominal and pelvic contractions.
- Humphrey/Limón (named after Doris Humphrey and José Limón) explores use of energy in relation to gravity and working with weight in terms of fall, rebound, recovery and suspension. Limón technique tends to use the feeling of weight and 'heavy energy' in the body.
- Release puts emphasis on minimizing tension in the search for clarity and fluidity and efficient use of energy and breath. In Release technique, the dancers release through the joints and muscles to create ease of movement, and show a greater sense of gravity.

(www.scottisharts.org.uk/1/artsinscotland/dance/features/
archive/stylecontemporarydance.aspx)

The Hong Kong Academy of Performing Arts is a good example of a higher education institution that is aware of the global opportunities for its dance graduates: it advertises on its website that:

> one of the primary features of the school is its emphasis on integration of all of the courses through the contextualisation of performance practice into wider artistic, theoretical and socio-cultural frameworks. Thus integration occurs through the three major study areas of Ballet, Chinese Dance and Contemporary Dance; across practical and theoretical studies; across creative and performance practice; across undergraduate and postgraduate activity; and across eastern and western practices. Every advantage is also taken of the unique east–west nexus that lies at the heart of Hong Kong culture.
>
> (www.hkapa.edu/asp/dance/dance_introduction.asp)

The Los Angeles Ballet Academy links all these together:

> 'Contemporary' is the name given to a group of 20th century concert dance forms. It is a collection of systems and methods

developed from Modern and Post-modern dance, thus contemporary dance is not a specific dance technique. Contemporary dance principles include: centering, alignment, gravity, breath, contraction, release, fall and recovery, suspension, balance and off-balance, tension and relaxation, opposition and emotion.

(www.laballet.com/classes/contdanceprog/index.html)

These four techniques are next described in a little more detail. Further reading on each is listed at the end of the chapter.

GRAHAM-BASED TECHNIQUES

Martha Graham said of her own technique: 'The spine is your body's tree of life. And through it a dancer communicates; his body says what words cannot, and if he is pure and open, he can make of his body a tragical instrument' (Graham, 1991: 8).

'Movement never lies', Graham was fond of saying. Her choreographies tended to explore 'deep matters of the heart' and her characters portray their internal experience, projecting their thoughts and feelings. The technical training which she evolved for herself and then for her dancers was selected from a set of fundamental principles: 'the contraction and the release; the spiral; the primacy of the central body in initiation movement, and the sequential growth of movement from the center of the body to the periphery' (Foster, 1986: 28). The daily class consists of a progression of well-defined exercises, starting with floor work, then centre work, then travelling sequences and finally very specific jumps which cross the floor. The class is infused with a full range of dynamic qualities – including percussive or elastic, with tension or suspension – and physical effort.

Jacqueline Smith-Autard (2002: 163) (in *The Art of Dance in Education*) describes a specific example of Graham technique being taught in a Dance degree course:

> Dance technique and performance modules in year 1 take the form of study of the technique devised by Martha Graham. This has been selected as the initial foundation upon which understanding of today's contemporary dance can be built. Students participate in rigorous technical classes to acquire dance skills

and Graham-based contemporary vocabulary. The class content – floor work, centre practice and travelling – culminates in sequences and style studies through which students become acquainted with the style and become able to perform longer pieces in a Graham-based technique. Performance skills, such as alignment, focus, projection, rhythm, musicality and expression, are practised and improved. The underlying principles and theories of the technique are studies through reading and writing assignments. Assessments take the form of classwork, short style studies, longer dances choreographed to include a range of Graham-based techniques and opportunities for the students to demonstrate their performance skills and written work.

Today, most university programmes in Dance offer more generic 'modern classes' at various levels, taught by various members of faculty, though the competences and the logical structure of the class are of course maintained.

HUMPHREY AND LIMÓN

Doris Humphrey's approach to the movement of the human body and its training was initiated more by an understanding of philosophy than by emotions. She had an enquiring and scientific mind, and it is said that her ideas about dance were stimulated by the writings of the nineteenth-century philosopher, Nietzsche. She observed nature and the human body, and was fascinated by Nietzsche's writings on the Greek deities Apollo and Dionysus, representing the two conflicting yet intertwining impulses in human beings. Apollo was the god of wisdom and light, measured and rational, whereas Dionysus, god of wine, song, dance and drama, was seen as releasing man's instinct for danger and adventure. Humphrey linked these thoughts to the notion of counterpoint in equilibrium: excitement and danger (off balance, out of control) on the one hand, symmetrical balance and repose on the other. We can see that the human body needs both these states, which is where the Humphrey principle of 'Falling and Recovering' comes from.

Her dance training was essentially derived from the basic motions of breathing, standing, walking, running, leaping, rising and falling: 'Since my dance is concerned with immediate human values, my basic technique lies in the natural movements of the human body' (Humphrey in Stodelle, 1979: 17).

As Stodelle (1979) describes, the dance technique of Doris Humphrey is built on the interrelationship of human movement and gravity to create motion. The principles of her movement language are based on the following elements: fall and recovery, successional flow, breath rhythms, oppositional motion, and change of weight. She always stressed that training should aim first at feeling for movement in design, in rhythm, in quality. Exercises in the form of studies explore thematic development and kinetic impulse.

> The structure of a Humphrey class is divided into four sections, starting with center work, then floor work, then barre work and spatial sequences. Within each section, elementary exercises progress to complex studies, aligned to the students' capabilities to absorb and express the characteristics of the technique.
>
> (Stodelle, 1979: 31)

José Limón (1908–1972) was another important figure in the development of this strand of modern dance: his powerful dancing shifted perceptions of the male dancer, while his choreography continues to bring a dramatic vision of dance to audiences around the world. In 1946, after studying and performing for 10 years with Doris Humphrey and Charles Weidman, he established his own company with Humphrey as Artistic Director.

Limón technique, based on that of Humphrey, emphasizes the natural rhythms of fall and recovery and the interplay between weight and weightlessness to provide dancers with an organic approach to movement that easily adapts to a range of choreographic styles (www.limon.org).

Daniel Lewis was a member of the José Limón Dance Company from 1962 to 1974. In 1999 he published *The Illustrated Dance Technique of Jose Limon*, detailing its history and philosophy, and describing preparatory exercises that teach the fundamentals of this dance technique, a breakdown of essential exercises, and a complete class beginning with floor work and progressing to centre exercises and across-the-floor combinations.

HAWKINS

Erick Hawkins was born in Colorado and studied at Harvard, where he majored in Greek civilization. Classical Greece became one of four great cultural influences on his work, the others being the Native American ideal, Japanese aesthetics and Zen. He was influenced by a performance by the German expressionist dancers Harald Kreutzberg and Yvonne Georgi, and after graduating in 1930 Hawkins spent two months in Austria studying with Kreutzberg. Later he studied at the School of American Ballet in 1934, danced with the American Ballet (the first company organized by George Balanchine and Lincoln Kirstein) from 1935 to 1937, and then with Kirstein's Ballet Caravan.

Hawkins met Martha Graham at Bennington College; in 1938, when she invited him to appear as a guest artist in *American Document*, he became the first man to dance with her company and the following year he officially joined it as her partner. He created leading roles in such important Graham works as *El Penitente* (1940), *Deaths and Entrances* (1943), *Appalachian Spring* (1944) and *Night Journey* (1947). Hawkins and Graham were married in 1948 and divorced six years later.

After leaving the Graham troupe in 1951, Hawkins formed his own small ensemble and began to develop his own style. He was an intensely musical choreographer who paid great attention to rhythm and dynamics. He redefined dance technique according to newly understood principles of kinesiology, creating a bridge to later somatic studies. Hawkins's famous statement was 'The body is a clear place.' His Normative Theory of Movement led to body movement which was free, simple, natural and unforced. Despite the soft, fluid, serene, almost effortless look, Hawkins's movement required substantial strength and specialized technique. Taking a released and sustained approach to the basics of Graham technique, he created a technique known for its 'directed, free flow of movement initiating from the center', according to Renata Celichowska, author of *The Erick Hawkins Modern Dance Technique* (2000). She describes its hallmarks as 'lightness, varied dynamics and clarity. Putting these qualities together is Hawkins' great contribution to dance training'.

A cluster of fundamental principles underlies the technique. The key concept behind a Hawkins dancer's unbound, soft-muscled quality is the notion of contraction and de-contraction. This does not imply movement that is not performed fully; rather, it suggests using only the effort required to perform efficiently. Hawkins declared that 'Tight muscles cannot feel. Only effortless, free-flowing muscles are sensuous.' The author Carrie Stern (2007) writes that Hawkins's principles include initiating and controlling movement from the body's pelvic centre of gravity; swinging the legs from high in the hip socket to activate lightness and freedom; finding the body's midline through the spine's four curves – cervical, thoracic, lumbar and sacral – allowing for efficient spinal alignment; pelvic pathways following under and over curves; and momentum recognized in curves, loops and spirals. The critic Molly McQuade notes that these principles develop dancers who, even when not literally leaping, soar 'indirectly, through furtive delicacy based on asymmetrical patterning; balances that look natural yet are not taken for granted; an energetic attitude of being held in suspension' (quoted in Stern, 2007). This sensation of flight, shared with the audience, is a Hawkins signature.

CUNNINGHAM

> If a dancer dances – which is not the same as having theories about dancing or wishing to dance or trying to dance or remembering in his body someone else's dance – but if the dancer dances, everything is there.... Our ecstasy in dance comes from the possible gift of freedom, the exhilarating moment that this exposing of the bare energy can give us. What is meant is not license, but freedom.
>
> (Cunningham, 1952)
> www.merce.org/about/biography.php.

Cunningham's first solo dance concert as choreographer was a shared programme with John Cage in 1944. He began to choreograph and work with his own dancers after working for several years (1939–1945) with Graham (see Chapter 3 below). He aimed for a modernism that was not anti-ballet, as was so much of modern dance. He desired to combine what he saw as the pronounced use of legs in ballet techniques with the strong emphasis on the spine and upper body that he had experienced in modern dance methods

(Grescovitch in Bremser, 1999: 73). He devised a new method of training the body which included standing exercises which stress five different positions of the back: upright, curve, arch, twist and tilt. This was based on the conviction that there should be a strong connection between the spine and legs, particularly the lower spine, so that when a dancer bends over, there is no sense of 'letting go' in order to counterbalance; rather, the legs are freed by the control of the spine. His dancers combined strong balance and flexibility in the legs with an articulate torso and speed and lightness of quality. While staying with a dance-technical idiom, he combined the elegant poise and brilliant footwork of ballet with the flexibility of spine and arms that Graham and her contemporaries had practised.

> Added to this synthesis of styles were Cunningham's own contri- butions: clarity, serenity, sensitivity to a wide range of speeds and sustainment in deploying steps and gestures, and the unusual qualities of isolation derived from chance combinations. The technical inventions and freedom of choreographic design create a style of dancing that seems to embody flexibility, freedom, change and ... pleasure in the idiosyncratic drama of individuality.
>
> (Banes, 1987: 9)

Cunningham's technique supports his vision of dance through its investigation of the body's possible movement. A technique class with Cunningham begins with exercises that thoroughly warm the muscles of the back and legs, explore the range of motion of each joint and establish basic patterns of movement for spine and arms, hips and legs, head and torso. Legs are firmly planted on the floor while the back exercises are done; then he alternates with leg exer- cises, and gradually develops the connection between spine and legs. Quite quickly, combinations of movements are introduced which challenge either the sense of timing or one's orientation in space, or both. The weight of the body shifts in combination with sudden changes of direction; large movements of the whole body are coor- dinated with smaller isolations, and there is little sense of flow to the whole sequence. The class uses no barre or floor work; the centre standing exercises become increasingly complex as turning and jumping are gradually introduced. New material is constantly being introduced; students have to absorb long sequences and remember them, but the next minute the timings and the spatial orientation could be adapted or changed. The pianist might change time-signature and the teacher might ask the dancer to make several different directional changes at the same time. Body and mind together master these movements, as Foster (1986: 35) describes.

Cunningham-based dance techniques are today offered in countries all over the world in the university sector and in professional dance schools. They may not be as 'pure' as some of us experienced with Merce Cunningham himself at the studio in Westbeth in New York City, for as students develop their own practices and move on to become instructors and choreographers, we find that the general principles are fused with an element of creative licence, and that this technique continues to evolve.

RELEASE-BASED

Release technique is an umbrella term that encompasses a variety of different corporeal practices that emphasize efficiency of movement. Emphasis is placed on breath, skeletal alignment, joint articulation, ease of muscular tension and the use of gravity and momentum to facilitate movement. In 1937, Mabel Elsworth Todd published *The Thinking Body*, introducing ideas about creative visual imagery and conscious relaxation to develop refined neuromuscular coordination. Her work influenced many physiology, dance and health professionals, and led to the development of the term 'idiokinesis' by Lulu Sweigard.

Another generic term used is 'somatic techniques' (soma meaning 'living, aware, bodily person'). Through the concept of 'soma', we understand that neither body nor mind is separate from the other; both are part of a living process. Many of the approaches in the field of somatics address the body–mind split endemic in Western culture; body–mind internal experience of the body is valued alongside an objective, analytical outside view of it.

Thomas Hanna used the term 'somatics' in the 1970s to describe various approaches to body–mind integration which he and others were developing. He describes as 'The art and science of the inter-relational process between awareness, biological function and environment, all three factors being understood as a synergistic whole' (1988). It is a method for reawakening the mind's control of movement, flexibility and health, and the subjective experience of the individual is considered important. The act of exploring and experiencing one's inner world through sensory awareness and integration is a means of understanding and engaging the impulse towards health and wellbeing (www.somaticsed.com).

For a dancer, the ability to develop sensory awareness, flexibility and fluidity in body movement is key to utilizing the body wisely and effectively; unfortunately, experiments indicate that the majority of young people entering Dance programmes in higher education arrive with problems associated with poor alignment, over-developed muscles or too much tension in the body. In release techniques, therefore, movement exercises are often designed to mirror and influence the natural processes of the body and mind, providing a fluid interconnection between movement, sensation and thought. Habitual or unhealthy patterns of being and experiencing oneself in the body can be released, helping students to trust in their inherent body wisdom. As perceptual, postural and movement interaction improves, better motor function and neo-cortex facility are achieved. Experiences which help to develop structural, functional and expressive integration serve as a form of self-education and self-development, which counter the norms of other forms of technical training where the student might be so overly concerned with the requirements set by the teacher in class that sensations and feelings are obscured.

Somatic theories are applied in somatic psychology, somatic movement and therapy, somatic body work and dance. Many dance departments in universities and colleges recognize the value of these practices and now ensure that students are introduced to greater kinaesthetic awareness of the body through one or more of the many techniques that have been developed: Alexander Technique, Feldenkrais, Pilates, yoga, tai chi, rolfing (structural integration), Skinner release, body–mind centring, idiokinesis, Laban Movement Analysis or Bartenieff Fundamentals.

For example, body mechanics concentrates on alignment of the body, balance and correct posture. Practice and knowledge of the alignment of shoulder girdle and pelvic girdle, and optimal joint movement, can aid the prevention of injury, whether one is working as a nurse, as a physiotherapist or as a dancer. Understanding the mechanics of force and motion, the place of gravity and how these regulate human movement is of value to all performers, whether sportsmen and women, actors or dancers. In gyms and health clubs worldwide, such mind–body exercise methods introduce members of the general public to the principles of alignment, posture, coordination, flexibility, lengthening and strengthening, articulation, breathing and the development of core strength.

As students in training, you will be able to follow the relationship of these release techniques not only to greater awareness of your own body, but also to their usage in therapeutic contexts, in their philosophy and practice in yoga and martial arts, and in the ways in which they have influenced post-modern and independent dance practices.

The objectives of these modules is to develop the ability to improvise freely and creatively from fundamental principles of motion and anatomical imagery; to create relaxed yet dynamic dancing; and to integrate strength, alignment, articulation and ease of movement. For example, you may learn the basics of Contact Improvisation and discover the need to be alert and attentive when working with a partner, but at the same time using economical tension and relaxation, maintaining alignment and posture, using gravity and momentum, showing sensitivity and safe practice in touching, rolling, lifting, weight bearing and balance.

FUSION AND HYBRIDITY

Every dance technique can be described as a philosophy, a theory and a series of practices. Dance techniques concern themselves in myriad ways with the study of the human body and its architecture, its functions and its capabilities, with extension, flow of energy, balance, coordination, etc. Essentially movement is based in the acts of breathing, standing, walking, running, rising and falling, turning and elevation. It is limited by the function of our body parts, our joints and sinews, and by our ability to defy gravity or give in to it.

Technique indicates the methods used to extend the natural movement capacities of the human body, dependent upon the ways in which the sub-discipline or choreographer wishes to use the body, modified by its use of space, variety of dynamic, and interaction with other bodies in time and space.

Some techniques like classical ballet educate the body to defy gravity, to defy natural turnout and to strengthen the feet and legs sufficiently to be able to leap, travel and rise on pointe. Others, like the Graham and Limón techniques, prepare for the act of moving through space by engaging with floor exercises first, to make spine, torso and legs stronger and more flexible. Techniques can be devised and developed by individual choreographers for the purpose of enabling dancers to perform their works as they are imagined, whereas others derive from social, ritual or urban dance forms or meditative forms like yoga or tai chi chuan. Through globalization, practice and the advent of scientific research, dance techniques have been developed, appropriated and fused into hybrid forms. Consider the martial art form called Kalaripayattu which has informed the work of choreographers such as Chandralekha and Shobana Jeyasingh, or Butoh, the Japanese form which has evolved through its connections with other performance arts and is now taught and practised in many countries (see for example, http://butoh.net).

Some dancers train only in one technique, while others embrace the flexibility of being able to perform in a variety of genres and styles. This might depend on the requirements of a particular company or on the personal philosophy, body shape or individual quality of the dancer. As a student in Dance in higher education you will be introduced to a number of ways of moving, and as you progress through your course, your personal preferences, together with your developing knowledge and aspirations for your future, will determine your approach to dance technique.

KINESIOLOGY AND INJURY PREVENTION

The study of human motion and injury prevention are traditionally found in the physical education departments of colleges and universities, but dancers also need to be made aware of the potential problems that can arise from ignorance, unsafe practice or overuse. Courses in a fine arts curriculum or performing arts department can be complemented by study units in biology, anatomy or physiology, and dance technique lecturers should be able to inculcate many of these principles in their classes.

Any kinesiology class should introduce understanding of the skeletal structure, the major classifications of joints, an awareness of muscle actions and characteristics, and the basic principles of flexion and extension, abduction and adduction, inward and outward rotation. Dancers need to understand the body in terms of:

- alignment, postural awareness and core stability – the architecture of the body;
- flexibility, elasticity, mobility and muscular balance;
- strength and stamina, endurance, conditioning and the cardio-vascular system;
- coordination and technical skill, energy, balance and accuracy: the nervous system;
- general body maintenance: health, diet/nutrition.

Since the various dance genres place different demands on the body, students cannot rely solely on the information presented by each technique teacher. The best way forward is to develop (throughout your programme) a sense of personal responsibility for your own body, informed by knowledge of the physical structures of the muscular-skeletal system and their functional relationships to the movements of the human body.

There are on the market some excellent texts to help this endeavour: for example, Blandine Calais-Germain's *Anatomy of Movement* (2007) and Eric Franklin's *Conditioning for Dance* (2004) are both written by experts who have years of practical experience in dance combined with in-depth scientific and anatomical knowledge. Both have worked consistently for many years with professional dancers to help them gain deeper kinaesthetic understanding of the internal structures of their bodies and the strength and flexibility necessary to improve their dance techniques.

HEALTH AND FITNESS

The body needs food for energy, growth and repair and to function properly and be healthy. This is especially important for a dancer. A regular diet of a high proportion of wholegrain products, fruit and vegetables and a low proportion of fat and sugars will provide your body with good nutrition and high energy levels.

The nutrients your body needs are carbohydrates, protein, fatty foods, fibre, vitamins and minerals.

- Carbohydrates are broken down into glucose, which is either used as energy or stored as glycogen in the liver and muscles. Complex carbohydrates are made up of sugar molecules strung together in long, complex chains and are in foods such as potatoes, pasta, rice and wholegrain breads. Simple carbohydrates are made up of processed and refined sugars, which provide energy but have little or no nutritional value, like sweets or fizzy drinks. Dancers should eat complex carbohydrates to provide plenty of energy.
- Protein is used to build and repair cells and is provided by foods such as meat, fish, soya and dairy products. Too little protein can cause haemoglobin levels in the blood to fall, which affects the body's stamina. Haemoglobin is a protein found in red blood cells.
- Your body needs some essential fatty acids, though they should be limited. A good source of these is oily fish, such as mackerel.
- Your body does not absorb fibre but it helps to keep the digestive system and heart healthy. Fibre is found in fruit and vegetables and wholegrain cereals such as rice bran and wheat cereals.
- The many different vitamins and minerals help your body to stay healthy, function properly and fight disease. It is better to get these from a balanced, varied diet than from supplements. Fruit and vegetables are good sources of vitamins and minerals.

More information on a healthy diet can be found at the website for the British Nutrition Foundation (www.nutrition.org.uk), the Nutrition Australia website on (www.nutritionaustralia.org) and www.Nutrition.gov in the USA.

The best way to have a healthy, nutritious diet is to eat a variety of foods and have regular meals and healthy snacks. You should ensure that you drink enough water to keep hydrated. Dancers in training also need sufficient rest, a healthy body weight, awareness of the capabilities and weaknesses of their own bodies, and understanding of the warning signs of fatigue. Take responsibility for your own body through becoming more educated, and carry these self-help tools with you as you progress through your dance training.

FURTHER READING/RESEARCH

Look up all the practitioners and genres/styles mentioned on www.
youtube.com.

Bales, M. and R. Nettl-Fiol (2008) *The Body Eclectic: Evolving Practices in Dance Training* Champaign, Ill.: University of Illinois Press

Cleney, G. (2003) *Basic Concepts in Modern Dance: A Creative Approach* Princeton, NJ: Princeton University Press

Freedman, Russell (1998) *Martha Graham: A Dancer's Life* New York: Clarion Books

Horosko, Marian (2002) *Martha Graham: The Evolution of Her Dance Theory and Training*. Gainesville, Fl.: University Press of Florida

Kostelanetz, Richard (ed.) (1992) *Merce Cunningham: Dancing in Space and Time* London: Dance Books

Nicholais, A. and M. Louis (2005) *The Nicholais/Louis Dance Technique: A Philosophy and Method of Modern Dance* London and New York: Routledge

2

MAKING DANCES

WHAT BASIC SKILLS/KNOWLEDGE DO DANCE-MAKERS REQUIRE?

Until the twentieth century, dance tended to be created instinctively by talented individuals, and often followed the structure of a narrative or a musical form. However, during the first half of the century, theatrical dance started to expand in numerous directions, demonstrating radical differences in technique, style, form and content. This growth and experimentation brought about more intellectual effort and analysis, demonstrating new theories of choreography and craftsmanship. Today a number of books are available on the basic skills and knowledge that dance-makers require: from the USA, Doris Humphrey's *The Art of Making Dances* (1959), Blom and Chaplin's *The Intimate Act of Choreography* (1982) and Sandra Minton's *Choreography: A Basic Approach Using Improvisation* (1986, 1997). From the UK, Valerie Preston-Dunlop's book *Looking at Dances: A Choreological Perspective on Choreography* (1998) is on all the dance course reading lists and Jacqueline Smith-Autard's *Dance Composition* has now run to its sixth edition (2010).

Most of these texts divide the craft of choreography into sections which include what Humphrey calls 'the ingredients and the tools'. Each dance has its own vocabulary, syntax, grammar and phrasing, but it will become evident (Chapter 3) that what interested one generation of choreographers soon became uninteresting to the next. As the discipline evolved, ideas about dance-making were continually challenged; should dances have specific meaning, as in character or plot, or could they be abstract? Is it best to use the stage space like a pretty picture, possibly symmetric, with everyone dancing together, or to deliberately challenge old rules of design in favour of individual material being performed anywhere on stage with an ethos of cooperative coexistence?

These textbooks tend to introduce the student to specific crafting ideas from different perspectives in logical progression, and then to trial some of the 'toolbox' of composition in short studies, experimenting alone or in small groups. The general stages of choreographic process mentioned include choosing a theme or stimulus, generating some dance vocabulary, developing the material using dynamics such as weight and time, and manipulating it in space. Natural movement might be used as inspiration, but is often stylized in order to extend literal gesture along a continuum from representational movement that can easily be recognized by audiences, to highly stylized, symbolic dance vocabulary that allows the audience members a greater degree of interpretative freedom.

Next in these texts follows some consideration of construction and form in dance-making, which might include manipulation and orchestration of the dance material, the use of contrasts or rhythmic shifts, or opposition, repetition, development or transitional ideas. The reason for teaching dance compositional theories in Dance Studies is to familiarize students with this range of potential skills through practice, to help them identify specific methods drawn from historical and contemporary sources and to encourage a more personal approach to choreography as knowledge, skill and personal aesthetic develop through experience. We do this by increasing the difficulty and complexity of the tasks as the course progresses: for example, a short solo or duet of two minutes in year 1, to a small group work of five to eight minutes in year 2, to a larger ensemble dance lasting up to 15 minutes in years 3 or 4.

An interesting factor is that many professional choreographers, especially those well established in classical ballet or jazz dance, may not recognize some of these compositional tools, as they tend to be developed and used in modern and contemporary dance. But in Dance Studies courses around the world, it is now considered important to ensure that students learn how to compose, develop a 'toolbox' of choreographic crafting skills, and apply these in their own performance work and their teaching and workshops with groups. After all, dance is a developing discipline, offering work in performing, making, teaching, facilitating and managing dance activity; having multiple skills related to dance will ensure a better possibility of finding work in our chosen areas of the larger dance field, and ensure that we can fulfil a number of roles within it.

The next six sections examine more deeply the general stages of the choreographic process, a sort of step-by-step approach to making a dance. Most of these stages apply to the creative art-making process in dance, whether by professionals, amateurs or students.

STAGE 1: STIMULUS/CONCEPTION/ INTENTION

What are we going to dance about, and what is the starting point of a dance? It could be a story, a feeling, a movement or dance phrase, an image that inspires or a moment's experience. Dance-makers and choreographers have been inspired by particular pieces of music, by paintings or sculptures, by phenomena such as land-scape or water, by political ideas such as national identity or gender issues, or by a sense of self within a particular experience: being in love, walking on a beach or climbing a mountain. Any of these ideas, and thousands more, could provide an impulse. This initial starting point may become a stimulus for the dance, but many other decisions also have to made, for example: What kind of dance style will be used? Where is this new work going to be per-formed? Who is it going to be created for, and how does the cho-reographer begin to visualize the dance? In other words, what is the *context*? This first stage of the creative process might include choosing a piece of music or a composer to work with, or ideas about costume and design. All this creative work may happen in the imagination, well before the choreographer and dancers meet in the studio. But gradually, a strong sense of *intention* and *concept* may begin to materialize. The dance-maker formulates ideas that provide not only a starting point but a possible route for the journey ahead.

Let us consider some examples of these starting points and inten-tions from different dance forms, chosen from professional, educa-tional and community contexts:

- Motionhouse Dance Theatre, a UK-based company, created *Scattered* (2009). It is about water, our relationships with it and its vital presence in our lives. The trademark of the company is essentially athletic and intensely physical, with a vocabulary based on contact improvisation. According to Kevin Finnan, the Artistic Director, the aim of the work was to integrate dance, aerial work, music, film and graphics.
- *Rites* (1997), based on Stravinsky's *Rite of Spring* (1913) by the Australian Ballet in a collaboration with Bangarra Dance Theatre and choreographed by Artistic Director Stephen Page, demonstrates a deliberate meeting between indigenous Australian culture and Western contemporary dance, with a theme of reconciliation.
- Project Sally, a choreographic collective of Stephan Ernst, Caroline Ribbers and Ronald Wintjens based in The Netherlands, created *Super* (2006). This work was for young children, based on a supermarket theme with a set of huge commercial refrigerators and shopping trolleys, but deliberately used a very sophisticated and abstract contemporary dance language rather than a more usual representational or mimetic dance vocabulary.
- As part of the Urban Moves Dance Festival in Manchester, Resonance Dance created a piece called *Forgotten Ghosts* (2010) where elegant figures from the 1940s find themselves in the frenetic surroundings of Piccadilly Station, re-enacting their tales of love and longing against a background of escalators, platforms and shopping crowds. Here a hybrid dance language was based on the social dancers of the period interspersed with a more contemporary dance language, produced as a site-specific work in a large city railway station.

All these ideas provide a starting point, a rationale for the dance to be created, a possible style of movement, a possible theme or narrative. These notions may provide a stimulus for the choreographer or dance-making group to start generating some dance material, some vocabulary to be developed, dance phrases that can be used as building bricks for the piece as a whole.

STAGE 2: DANCE CONTENT: THE GENERATION OF LANGUAGE

Once a concept or intention has been decided and the dancers chosen, when rehearsals begin the choreographer needs to start making movement which will become the *language* of the dance. But is the language of a dance given or improvised? Is it a known vocabulary, a personal movement style or something completely new? And if new, how is it created?

There are many ways of making new dance material which can then be developed through orchestration or manipulation. Traditionally, the classical ballet idiom was codified in such a way that every step has a name, and teachers can combine these steps in a number of different ways to provide dance phrases or enchaînements in a ballet class. Classical choreographers can use the same methods to produce whole sections of ballets, combining steps like glissade, pas de bourrée, arabesque and pirouette in a flowing musical phrase. Like building sentences from words and phrases in your own language, everyone in the studio knows and understands how to perform this material; it is endemic to most ballet classes and can be performed in either simpler or more complex versions, but essentially it is based on a *given* language. Consider the language of Petipa/Ivanov's *Swan Lake* (1895) or Coralli/Perrot's *Giselle* (1845), as we might see it performed today, and compare it with the dance language of Balanchine's works for the New York City Ballet or the Bournonville romantic style of the Royal Danish Ballet. There are many stylistic variations, but some of the language will be common to all.

In other dance styles like modern and contemporary dance, choreographers have found different ways of moving the body and made new vocabulary in order to communicate their personal ideas. This means that instead of one codified technique or dance language, a wide range of styles has developed. For example, in Germany between the First and Second World Wars, Rudolf Laban made highly expressive, story-based dance-dramas from 1923 to 1927 with his company Kammertanzbühne Laban (Bradley, 2009: 18), whereas Kurt Jooss preferred themes that addressed moral issues. He synthesized naturalistic movements with a strong balletic training and characterization to address political concerns of the time. Jooss's most important choreographic work, *The Green Table* (1932), won first prize at an international competition for new choreography in Paris in 1932. It was a strong anti-war statement, created a year before Adolf Hitler became the Chancellor of Germany.

In America, the modern dance rebellion through the early twentieth century was led by Isadora Duncan, Loie Fuller, Ruth St Denis, Ted Shawn, Martha Graham, Doris Humphrey, Charles Weidman, José Limón and others who challenged European schools of dance and their conventions. Instead, they favoured the creation of dance forms which expressed the American heritage – expressive, communicative, related to the characteristics of the people or the landscape, the puritan or the primitive, Americana or religious themes, theatricality, humanity, reality. The dance languages created by these early modern dancer/choreographers were often characterized by movement initiated by the pelvis or spine, with a strong sense of gravity and flexibility, angularity and a strong dynamic, defying the lightness and ethereality of the romantic or classical ballet traditions. If we investigate the movement language of Martha Graham's *Lamentation* (1930) or *Cave of the Heart* (1946), or Doris Humphrey's *Water Study* (1928) or *Shakers* (1931), we find that the vocabulary was created by a dance-maker who was also a performer. Thus, it starts as a language of internal sensory communication, drawing on what Hawkins (1991: vii) describes as 'images, sensations, obscurities, emotions, intuitions, and biological factors of the individual'. In other words, the dance language is no longer a codified set of known and practised steps, learned from outside the dancer's own experience, but is developed internally from an intimate investigation of one individual's accumulated memories, thoughts and sensations, already sited in his or her own body.

The black American experience was expressed by such choreographers as Katherine Dunham, Pearl Primus, Alvin Ailey, Donald McKayle and Judith Jamieson who also drew on personal memory, sensations and intuitions, but beyond that on the African heritage, imagined and experienced, communicated by family and ancestors. For example, McKayle grew up in an integrated neighbourhood of New York, which helped to shape his understanding of the social issues and racial prejudices in America at a time when racism and segregation were commonplace. His choreography *Rainbow Round My Shoulders* (1959) incorporates Africanist movement, rhythms and music. Prisoners in a chain gang move powerfully across the stage, creating an expressive narrative through abstract movements of hard physical work. McKayle alludes to African American dreams of freedom and equality through his images of slavery and bondage. The racial injustice and violence of the piece concludes as a chain gang member is shot and killed. Ailey's seminal work *Revelations* (1960) tells the story of African American faith and tenacity from slavery to freedom through a suite of dances set to spirituals and blues music, and is still performed at the end of each programme of the Alvin Ailey American Dance Theater.

A radically different approach to the creation of dance language happened in New York in the 1960s, as a group of dancers who were interested in challenging the status quo started to develop different methods of generating dance content from scores, chance methods and such like. These methods took away the choreographer's responsibility to create appropriate movements to communicate the *theme* or *intention*. Instead, the group used methods like the I Ching, or dice or playing cards to generate new movement. In the 1950s, Merce Cunningham became interested in abstract or non-literal dance forms, which simply emphasized movement rather than representing any historical figure, emotional situation or idea. Chance operations provided him with an interesting approach, as he explains:

> John Cage and I became interested in the use of chance in the 50's. I think one of the very primary things that happened then was the publication of the *I Ching*, the Chinese book of changes, from which you can cast your fortune: the hexagrams.
>
> Cage took it to work in his way of making compositions then; and he used the idea of 64 – the number of the hexagrams – to say that you had 64, for example, sounds; then you could cast, by chance, to find which sound first appeared, cast again, to say which sound came second, cast again, so that it's done by, in that sense, chance operations. Instead of finding out what you think should follow – say a particular sound – what did the I Ching suggest? Well, I took this also for dance.
>
> I was working on a title called, 'Untitled Solo', and I had made – using the chance operations – a series of movements written on scraps of paper for the legs and the arms, the head, all different.
>
> (Cunningham, 2000)
> http://en.wikipedia.org/wiki/Merce_Cunningham

Although at that time the use of chance operations was considered an abrogation of artistic responsibility, Cunningham was thrilled by a process that arrives at works that could never have been created through traditional collaboration.

Generating dance content through chance methods

What effect does the use of charts, scores and chance procedures have on choreography and on the norms of the choreographic process? We know that Cunningham believed in dances which were 'virtually devoid of "expressive" or "symbolic" elements. He also insisted on "freeing" choreography from its dependence on music' (Copeland in Copeland and Marshall, 1983: 311).

For many choreographers, chance techniques offer the possibility of freeing ourselves from the habits that have been conditioned. For student groups, using chance methods can be a fun, liberating and innovative way of generating unusual movement. It can demonstrate how quickly new sequences can be made and manipulated, in a 'workmanlike' way, without the kind of personal involvement that other forms of crafting require. Scores that I have worked on as a teacher include Remy Charlip's *Five Twos*, Trisha Brown's *Cube* and Yvonne Rainer's *Horst* solo. I have also created charts, such as simple squares on a large piece of paper, filled with different dynamic qualities, or actions of the body, or spaces in the room, and asked the students to toss coins to choose what and how and where to dance! Students have created quite complex charts using packs of cards, dice or roulette wheels. We make new material, then use other chance methods to determine who dances with whom, or what music to use: it is quite fascinating to see how different types of music – classical, jazz, pop or rap – affect a phrase of dance. We find ourselves asking how this kind of work affects the spectator's perceptual freedom? Or does it just impede or deny the sensory pleasure that dance can provide? Do audiences need to know *how* the dance has been created in order to appreciate it?

From the 1960s, on both sides of the Atlantic, such post-modern ideas took hold and dance vocabulary was borrowed from all kinds of 'other' movement forms not normally seen on the dance concert stage: various forms of martial arts were appropriated, including tai chi, aikido and capoeira. Some dancer/choreographers chose to demystify the body by putting everyday gestures and pedestrian movement on stage, or to borrow all kinds of movements and steps from social dance forms, sometimes mixing them up indiscriminately. Dance practitioners like Steve Paxton introduced Contact Improvisation, exploring the parameters of the basic duet form for a group of men without 'dancerly' movement:

> What happens when the partners give weight, lift, carry, wrestle each other, give in to the floor and gravity, all in a way that breaks out of typical male habits of aggression or fear of tenderness?... [Contact Improvisation] is a movement that originates in a variety of duet situations, ranging from handshakes to making love to brawling to social dancing to meditation.
>
> (Banes, 1987: 64–65)

So we can see that so-called dance material can be codified, or created from within, or borrowed, or amalgamated in a variety of different ways. It can be already existing or given; it can be improvised by the choreographer or by the dancers in collaboration: it can be stylistically coherent or not, depending on the circumstance. In the present day, many choreographers prefer to set tasks for their dancers to respond to, thus allowing them to contribute artistically to the dance-making process. In the next section, we investigate these processes of making more closely. But, first, let us go back to some basic approaches to creating a vocabulary for dance that we might also encounter in the Dance Studies discipline.

Improvising to create new language

In Blom and Chaplin's book *The Moment of Movement* (1988), which offers a comprehensive and thoughtful approach to the art of movement improvisation, the authors define 'improvisation in dance' as follows:

> Dance improvisation fuses creation with execution. The dancer simultaneously originates and performs movement without preplanning. It is thus creative movement of the moment. [It]

is a way of tapping the stream of the subconscious without intellectual censorship, and allowing spontaneous and simultaneous exploring, creating and performing.

(1988: x)

Of course, one of the issues about allowing the body to perform 'movement without preplanning' is that our bodies are already constructed by our experiences in our formative years, our culture (i.e. country, class, gender, age), by our personal philosophies and beliefs *and* by any previous training – issues that will be further discussed in Chapter 5 below. Indeed, your dancing body may already signify to others such details as

- where you come from;
- what your attitudes are; or
- what kind of previous training you have experienced.

However, improvisation can also be used to develop kinaesthetic awareness, engage in the creative process, increase awareness of self, free the body from its learned responses, or to learn how to initiate and respond to movement and dance 'in the moment'. Two further important uses of dance improvisation, now well documented, are improvisation in performance (that is, creating movement in the moment, watched by an audience) and improvisation as a tool for generating dance content in composition, as a form of initial exploration in movement to try to physically encapsulate the imagined emotions, imagery or inspirations from our starting point.

We might improvise and experiment in the studio to find movement which feels right, which expresses the dance-maker's images, which seems to be relevant to the idea for the dance, and which has the potential for development. Once this has been selected and refined, Smith-Autard (2010: 40) calls this movement or movement phrase 'the motif', something which is sufficiently interesting to be capable of being developed. In Dance Studies, 'developing the motif' is one of the valuable choreographic tools which raises students' awareness of the myriad ways of creating a dance, and therefore it is usually introduced early in a programme (see next section).

Dance students need to experience a range of creative processes, with the awareness of what we mean by 'creativity', and with growing understanding of what other authors have written about the phases of art-making. Rollo May (1975, 1995) identifies four phases, which he calls:

- preparation
- exploration
- illumination
- formulation

where 'exploration' might be the 'improvisation' phase in dance creation, whereas Peter Abbs (1989: 204) suggests five phases, which he demonstrates in spiral form:

- expressive impulse
- working within the medium
- realization of final form
- presentation and performance
- response and evaluation.

In Abbs's chart, 'working with the medium' probably relates to the improvisation phase. Usually, Bachelor or Bachelor of Fine Arts Dance degrees include modules or study units called Dance Improvisation, or Improvisation and Performance, Fundamentals of Choreography or Dance Practice, Choreographic Approaches or Dance Composition, where students are introduced to the norms of the discipline and are also encouraged to find new ways of generating and developing content, structuring and forming to create dances, either in solo, duet or group work.

STAGE 3: PROCESSES AND MODES OF MAKING

Here, the choreographer needs to consider the context of the dance-making process, e.g. whether it is for a professional company, a community or amateur group, or an educational situation. Another important facet of dance-making is about how it is to be managed and led. That is, within the artistic process of making a dance, what possible dancer–choreographer relationships can be employed, and what does each of them offer? By understanding a range of approaches available in the creation of choreography, students can appreciate distinct dancer–choreographer relationships and their impact on dance creation. We cannot assume for example that all choreographers wish to adopt a dictatorial role, despite the fact that tradition maintains that a *ballet master* was in command of all artistic decision-making. Some choreographers, like Frederick Ashton, would prepare the overall structure of a new work, familiarize himself with the music and/or text, and imagine tableaux and designs on stage, but he only started to choreograph in any detail within the studio with dancers. He has stated in interview, 'I never choreograph until I'm with people … I might have certain ideas but I don't do steps till then … so I do make a certain structure' (1984: 2–7). Farjeon describes the 'stillness and silence' in the studio on the days when Ashton had no ideas, or when he challenged the dancers to dance something which would get him started. He would play and experiment with shapes, and manipulate his dancers to create images; 'on other occasions he knew just what he wanted, but movements were always open to improvements' (Farjeon in Carter and O'Shea, 2010: 26).

One famous example of a choreographer who arrived in the studio with many of her decisions already made was Ninette de Valois (later to be Director of the Royal Ballet):

> At the first rehearsal de Valois would remain cool, concentrated and often humorous. She was already primed with ideas and knew what she wanted: it had already been written down in a notebook. Save for a pianist or merely using the score, she had marked out the details of the whole ballet in private. She inclined to use dancers as puppets to be manipulated and there was little elasticity to the system. Now and then she would alter some step, rearrange a pattern, or bring a character more to the fore, but it was seldom necessary. Her private imaginings had been pretty accurate.
>
> (Farjeon in Carter and O'Shea, 2010: 24)

To help student dancers to become aware of these different artistic and social approaches to working in the studio, my didactic-democratic framework model (Butterworth, 2004, 2009) provides five distinct approaches to the generic choreographic process (see Figure 2.1). It can also help choreographers, teachers and dance workers to

Process 1	Process 2	Process 3	Process 4	Process 5
Choreographer as expert	Choreographer as author	Choreographer as pilot	Choreographer as facilitator	Choreographer as co-owner
Dancer as instrument	Dancer as interpreter	Dancer as contributor	Dancer as creator	Dancer as co-owner
Didactic processes ←———————————————————————→ Democratic processes				

Figure 2.1 Butterworth's didactic–democratic model (2009).

- identify their personal preferences;
- recognize the specific needs of participants in the application of choreographic skills; and
- modify rehearsal processes to take into consideration the needs of the participants.

The model identifies five different artistic-social processes that can be utilized in the dance studio during the course of making a particular choreography or in learning about choreography. More detail is published in a chapter in *Contemporary Choreography: A Critical Reader* (Butterworth and Wildschut, 2009: Chapter 12) as many university and colleague courses are now using and applying this model in some form in their composition and choreography modules.

The reason for introducing the model here is to identify clearly *how* the dance concepts and motifs are developed when we make dances. For example, is all the material created and taught by the choreographer in a didactic way? That is, where the *choreographer is seen as expert and the dancer is seen as an instrument* with the capability to imitate and replicate the dance material exactly as required? This method is clearly used in situations where students are studying syllabus work for an examination or where a dancer has to step in to an existing part in a finished choreography.

When a dancer is asked to learn a set piece of choreography but is allowed to bring a personal interpretation to it, then the choreographer-dancer relationship is more like that between an *author and an interpreter*; for example, if you are dancing with a company like Ballet Met Columbia or Northern Ballet, and have been given the title role in *Aladdin* (2008) or *Cleopatra* (2011), then the choreographer has chosen to work with *you* because of the personal abilities and qualities that you can bring to the role. Equally, if you are a first year/fresher student who has been chosen by a final year Dance student to perform in his or her choreography for assessment (or if you attend an audition and the choreographer has chosen you) then probably some special qualities have been recognized in the way you perform: your stage persona or particular physical attributes or skills have been acknowledged.

The third process is called *choreographer as pilot and dancer as contributor*; this occurs when the dancers or students receive set tasks or improvisations from the choreography, related to the aims of the choreography, and can be seen as an introduction to devising. The choreographer normally facilitates this by designing improvisatory tasks that fit in with his/her concept, and then by shaping, editing and developing the material that ensues. Of course, the dancers' contributions have to fit in with the dance concept, and will very likely be adapted and modified by the choreographer to ensure stylistic coherence. No dance-maker will want to adopt a long section of someone else's material into his or her dance. Nevertheless, the big advantage of working in this way is that the group feels as though everyone has some ownership of the making of the dance. In order to set up the task effectively, the 'pilot' needs to ensure that the dancers/students understand the intention and concept of the dance in order to contribute to it, while at the same time maintaining control of the overall devised piece. This process is often used in small ensemble dance company work where the choreographer leads, guides and trusts her dancers and where the dancers have great experience of working together. A good example of this trust can be demonstrated by the work of the British choreographer Siobhan Davies and her dance company, whose many works can be viewed in full on the web-based Siobhan Davies Archive (see www.siobhandaviesreplay.com).

The fourth process in the model is termed *choreographer as facilitator, dancer as creator*. Here the dancers truly collaborate with the choreographer, engage in the devising process, contribute to the creative process through negotiation, participate actively in content creation and decisions about structure, and fully interact with the group. The choreographer owns the concept, and has the right to make changes, veto decisions and control the overall structure of the work, making decisions about the scenographic elements and the coherence of the whole work. This is seen as an interactive process, where whoever is leading tends to nurture and mentor other members of the group. Examples can be found in small ensembles, community groups and student groups.

Finally, the fifth process means *sharing ownership* of work from research and intention to negotiation and decision-making, sharing participation on content creation and development, form and structure. This process usually refers to dancer-choreographers working in ensemble where they have chosen to share authorship, work democratically and interact quite equally across the group. A good example of this kind of work can be seen in the dance and theatre groups Frantic Assembly, DV8, Théâtre de Complicité and Grotest Maru based in Berlin.

STAGE 4: DANCE CONTENT DEVELOPMENT

In the next stage we focus on what can be done artistically with the chosen movement, what we might call the 'crafting'. Stage 4 of a choreographic process often, but not always, involves the development, orchestration and manipulation of the material created in Stage 2. There are many different approaches to crafting, some of them belonging to particular genres or styles of dance, others to a specific artistic period or an individual choreographer or teacher. As identified, this might be existing dance vocabulary that has been learned in class, or 'found' through improvisation, or created by the choreographer by small phrases or 'nuggets' of movement which are called 'motifs', capable of being developed, extended and otherwise orchestrated.

Let us start with a tried and tested method of developing new dance material based on a character from a play, film or novel. Imagine you want to make a dance based on the character of Lady Macbeth from Shakespeare's *Macbeth;* you would probably begin by reading the play or watching a film version, in order to see what happens to this woman; you would then discover that she is the wife of Macbeth, who in real life was considered an able, powerful king of Scotland. However, in Shakespeare's play, Macbeth first hears the three witches' prophecies proclaiming that he will one day be king. He tells his wife, Lady Macbeth, who hatches a plan to kill the present King Duncan, and secure the throne for her husband. Macbeth resists, but she challenges his manhood and he eventually follows her plan. Macbeth kills others who suspect him of wrongdoing, and takes the crown of Scotland as king. At a royal banquet, he plans to murder Banquo, a fellow general, and is later visited by Banquo's ghost, whom he fears.

Lady Macbeth becomes wracked with guilt for the crimes she and her husband have committed. She sleepwalks and tries to wash imaginary bloodstains from her hands, all the while speaking of the terrible things she knows. Lady Macbeth dies (it is not revealed how, but perhaps it is suicide), and Macbeth, now viewed by all as a tyrant, goes into battle again and is beheaded by Macduff.

The narrative gives some detail of the character of Lady Macbeth, but also leaves much that can be interpreted by a young choreographer: her pride, her arrogance, her accusatory bullying of her husband and her dream of being queen of Scotland. Later, after watching her husband terrified by the ghost of Banquo, she realizes what has been done; we imagine that she has nightmares, she sleepwalks, she feels guilt, trying to wash the imaginary signs of murder from her hands, and finally dies from we know not what.

How might we use these factors to make a solo dance? For example, first, imagine creating three or four motifs that indicate the initial moods and attitudes of Lady Macbeth; these might be quite mimetic or representational, made up of postures or quite literal gestures that communicate her power, her arrogance, her accusations or her dreams of sitting on the throne of Scotland with her husband. Next, imagine how she might feel when reality hits her – her realization of what she and her husband have done; recognition and shock as she sees her husband shouting at an empty chair, her nightmares and sleepwalking, her despair and her deep feelings of guilt.

Your first job might be to create and select these motifs, and to find ways of developing them (see, for example, Smith-Autard, 2010: 42–50). In terms of the construction of a dance, motifs need to be repeated, otherwise they tend to be forgotten, but they also need to be developed, to become more complex and elaborate through variation and contrast as the dance continues, otherwise they would get rather tedious. Think of dance 'motifs' as one of the building blocks of dance-making.

Next, consider the numerous possibilities for developing each of these 'nuggets' of material; think of the 'motif' as an organizing device for your dance. Just as a composer of music might establish a short melody that is developed, varied, extended, before he adds a new melody which might contrast or complement the first, the dance choreographer can establish a dance motif, develop or extend it so that the audience recognize it as a component of this particular dance.

How can we develop our movement 'nugget'? Perhaps through altering the rhythm or the size of the movement; by making changes to the dynamic quality of the movement, or its spatial level or direction; perhaps by using the 'nugget' as a starting point for initiating travelling, turning, leaping or changing its tempo from slow to fast, its flow from free to bound, or altering the degree of tension used to perform it.

Consider how Lady Macbeth might travel freely round the stage space in her confident or arrogant phase, but zigzag erratically in her later stages of despair; her floor pattern might modify and change in relation to her shifting mood and attitude. Imagine the pace of trying to wipe the metaphorical blood off your hands in panic, or tossing and turning in a nightmare of guilt. The movement might grow from a small gesture to an extended phrase, vary its quality of weight, speed or flow, or emphasize increasing asymmetry in the dancer's body as her guilt intensifies. In the construction of a dance we need to consider the possibilities of additions, repetitions or recapitulation, manipulation or 'remixing' of the movement material.

Now, let us imagine that you decide to create a longer dance with more performers; you need someone to play Macbeth, King Duncan, Banquo and Macduff, and perhaps other characters, and you have already created dance motifs for each of them, symbolizing their personal qualities. But you will also need to show interesting relationships and interactions between these dancers; for example, how might you present the three witches telling Macbeth that one day he will be king, and how do you think he would respond? In their various scenes together, Lady Macbeth and her husband seem to experience many moods, so how might you present the part where she manages to persuade Macbeth to kill the king, or the section where Macbeth is terrified by a vision of the ghost of Banquo, who he thought was dead? And most importantly, how can we develop these parts of our dance sufficiently so that recognizable movement or mimetic gestures become more dance-like? How can movement be manipulated?

This development stage uses many ideas to develop the *actions (what moves?)*, to introduce different *dynamics (how?)*, to explore how the body moves in *space (where?)*: most of the texts on composing dances (see Further Reading section at the end of this chapter) provide more detail on these elements, but we will briefly consider these one at a time.

Actions of the body

Human movement provides us with a great deal of information. When we observe people moving in the street or in a shopping centre we see specific actions related to posture, gesture, locomotion and stillness, and we can normally understand what is going on, at least in our own culture. Posture can communicate age, gender, attitude or pain; we read gestures, particularly of the hand, arm, head and shoulder, with no difficulty; we can travel by crawling, hopping, walking and running at different stages of our lives, and stillness might occur while waiting, spectating, talking or watching. In dance, these elements become the fundamental basic movement palette, with the addition of the actions of turning, elevation and falling. As dancers, we add to that palette from our knowledge of different dance genres and styles to provide more actions, steps, vocabulary to choose from.

Dynamics of the body

Again, human beings move with particular qualities which help us to recognize their moods, attitudes, personalities. We can observe the amount of energy or power that is being used, the control, the strength or weakness of a movement, its speed or weight or flow. Laban's analysis of movement qualities (of time, weight, space, flow) provide the choreographer with many choices. A movement can be performed at many different speeds, with a sense of strength or lightness, with a quality of flexibility or directness, or with free flow or more tension or control.

However, our choice has to be appropriate to the dance, to the character or mood being portrayed. If we are to find Lady Macbeth's movement believable, we might expect it to be radically different in the 'sleepwalk' scene from the controlled directness of her more confident moments. To depict a bad dream, or fear or panic, the quality of the dynamics would need to change and perhaps become more complex.

The body moving in space

First, consider two aspects of space: the space around the body, like a bubble, which Laban termed our personal kinesphere, and the larger space of the studio or stage which we share with fellow dancers. In our personal space the body can move in different directions (forwards, backwards, sideways, diagonally) and at different levels (high, medium and low), in curved, straight or angular shapes and with wide extensions or narrow contractions. We can distinguish the difference between moving symmetrically or asymmetrically in the dimensions or diagonals; an arm gesture pattern or a floor pattern can both be spatially defined.

Choreographers have a great deal of choice as to where they place dancers in the space and where they travel but they are also aware of the usual 'norms' of a particular dance style. In classical ballets which are based in narrative, plot and character, and where the traditional 'picture frame' proscenium arch stage is used, it is usual for the principal dancers to take specific roles (e.g. Romeo and Juliet, Don Quixote with Sancho Panza and Dulcinea, Cinderella and her prince, Cleopatra and Mark Antony) while the company provide the support, context and frame for those relationships. At the other end of the 'spatial' spectrum, post-modern dances often deliberately challenge this norm by climbing up walls (Trisha Brown), dancing in museums, galleries and gymnasia (Cunningham, Grand Union) or dancing in the street (Kenneth King, Lucinda Childs).

In Dance Studies, students learn about the importance of space through diverse experiences of making dance in different spaces and stages, of considering a range of aesthetic choices and of performing and analysing the dances of other choreographers. Much has been written in the textbooks about the 'power' of centre stage and the diagonal lines that cross it, about creating stage design or an environment, but these are not regulations, just possibilities. As students develop their understandings of the relationship of dance and space through both study and experimentation, the possibilities for new conceptions of space will grow.

For example, in classical ballet and early modern dance the space was usually observed in terms of a proscenium arch framing the stage. Dances tended to be frontal, with dancers facing the audience and projecting directly to them. Doris Humphrey's chapter on the uses of space in *The Art of Making Dances* (1959) reflects the tendency at that time to consider centre stage as the centre of interest. Merce Cunningham, however, decided to abandon that idea in favour of Einstein's notion of no fixed points in space – to believe that any place is as important as any other. Placing dancers all over the space facing different directions opens up a huge range of possibilities for choreographers, and challenges audiences to discover other ways of looking (see Chapter 3 below). Gradually, awareness and understanding of space has changed; and it is challenged even further when we examine site-specific dances (composed for a specific external or internal space) or indeed the use of video and other technologies (see Chapter 6 below).

Let us now turn to a completely different example of dance content development, where the intended outcome is to be abstract or non-literal, an approach to choreography that owes something to a pendulum swing away from the Freudian symbolism, social consciousness and emotional involvement of the first American modern dancers. In the 1940s and 1950s, a strong trend towards non-literal choreography became evident in the work of George Balanchine, Robert Joffrey, Alwin Nikolais, Paul Taylor and Merce Cunningham. Margery Turner defined non-literal dance as 'movement and motion', where dance concerns itself with 'feelings, attitudes, images, relationships, shapes and forms which can communicate directly through the senses' (1971: 3).

Like abstract art, where the spectator might be interested in the colour, shape and texture of a picture without knowing what it represents or caring what it *means*, non-literal dance can be created through exploration of mechanical laws of movement (gravity, balance, force, etc.) or through kinaesthetic sensing. It is removed from the human condition and from daily experience; but to the dancer and choreographer, the materials of the medium of movement are as interesting as colour and texture are to a painter or sounds to a musician.

A good example of one of the early non-literal choreographers is Alwin Nikolais:

> For nearly sixty years, Alwin Nikolais was modern dance's pioneer of multimedia. Among his best known performances are 'Masks, Props, and Mobiles' (1953), 'Totem' (1960), and 'Count Down' (1979). Nikolais would often present his dancers in constrictive spaces and costumes with complicated sound and sets, designed to confuse the process of dance. By placing obstacles in the dancers' way, he focused their attention on the physical tasks of overcoming those obstacles. Nikolais viewed the dancer not as an artist of self-expression, but as a talent who could investigate the properties of physical space and movement.
>
> (www.pbs.org/wnet/americanmasters/episodes/alwin-nikolais/about-alwin-nikolais/674)

Let us imagine this time that you have been asked to make a non-literal group dance with five dancers. You will still need to create some movement building blocks or 'nuggets' of material, but you will have much more freedom to make choices about how you develop this material, and design the dance in space. This time, two other elements become important; first, how will you deal will the relationship between the five dancers and, second, how might you 'orchestrate' the movement material?

Relationships between dancers

It is very rare and often rather tedious to make a dance that is always in unison; but unison can be very effective if used sparingly. Developing a dance with five different dancers is analogous with a very complex kind of knitting pattern, where the stitches might be different but they all eventually coalesce in the colourful patterns of the jumper. Other kinds of movements that can happen at the same time, or indeed in canon, are contrasting or complementary movements and background–foreground juxtaposition.

For example:

1 Dancer 1 dances the motif twice, once slowly (A) and then faster but in a different direction (A2).
2 Dancer 2 dances a variation of the motif (A3).
3 Dancer 3 dances the same variation but in canon with Dancer 2 (A3 delayed).
4 Dancer 4 dances a contrasting slower motif (B).
5 Dancer 5 dances the same contrasting slower motif in canon with Dancer 4 (B2).

If you visualize these instructions, you will recognize that three dancers start together, and two dancers join in later in an interesting juxtaposition of movement; simply by using unison, contrast, development and variation, it is possible to create a whole section of a dance based on just one motif. Within the same dance, you might deliberately have a section where one dancer performs a solo juxtaposed with a group of four; or three dancers provide a background section to contrast a unison section by two dancers in the foreground. Perhaps one dancer is performing a sequence of jumping while the other four dancers develop the phrase at floor level, then one of these four starts to reverse the phrase ... With a little imagination the opportunities for development and orchestration are endless. But at some point the choreographer needs to manipulate or edit each section of the dance as an entity with some coherence, and also to consider the overall structure of the dance.

Relationships of dance with music

How can the two disciplines of dance and music work together? Traditionally, as we are aware from studying classical and romantic ballet, there was usually a very close relationship between what was heard and what was danced until the twentieth century. Ballet masters often choreographed to pre-existing music (e.g. Petipa working with the music of Tchaikovsky), modern and contemporary dancers often worked closely with composers (e.g. Graham and Copland, Siobhan Davies and Kevin Volans, Mark Morris and cellist Yo-Yo Ma), and other contemporary choreographers have followed the Cunningham–Cage notion of 'peaceful coexistence'.

These relationships can be categorized in three broad ways:

1 dependent
2 interdependent
3 independent

Another way of conceptualizing these categories is that music and dance are 'married', 'separated' or 'divorced'. Let us look at these three relationships more deeply, and discuss some exemplars.

Many choreographers start by choosing a piece of music or by deciding to re-choreograph to an existing score. For example, many of Frederick Ashton's works were initiated by the choice of a piece of music that stimulated ideas and imagery for a new dance, e.g. *Symphonic Variations* (1946) to music by Cesar Franck, *The Dream* (1964) to Mendelssohn arranged by Lanchbery, or *Enigma Variations* (1968) to the suite by Edward Elgar.

First, what do we mean by dependent? This concept may be divided into at least three areas; for example, 'Mickey Mousing', music visualization and direct correlation. 'Mickey Mousing' is a term used in film, meaning to synchronize or mirror the music with the actions on screen. It comes from early Walt Disney films where the music reinforces an action by mimicking its rhythms exactly. In dance we use it to describe a situation where the dance effectively mimics the music, usually for humorous effect, as in the clog dance from *La Fille mal Gardée* (1960) with music by Hérold (arranged by Lanchbery), danced by the Widow Simone, a part always danced by a man, just as pantomime dames in English Christmas shows are always played by men. Here, music and dance support the inherent humour of a man dressed as a woman. It should be added that the term can also be used in a derogatory way when a dance-maker is too reliant on the rhythmic patterns of the music.

The term 'music visualization' was used as a descriptor of the solo performances of Isadora Duncan (the term was coined by Ruth St Denis) as she improvised in her natural, 'free' technique to composers such as Chopin, Gluck and Beethoven. In her own technique of dance composition, the movement grew out of emotions evoked by the music, or at other times the movement evolved, beginning as emotions expressed by gestures in silence, for which she would then select music that she thought illustrated those same emotions. Today, 'music visualization' is used to describe a feature found in electronic music visualizers and media player software, which generates animated imagery based on a piece of music. The imagery is usually generated and rendered in real time and synchronized with the music as it is played.

Other examples of choreographers who have chosen to work with existing ballet scores or other existing music include George Balanchine, Christopher Bruce, Paul Taylor, Mark Morris, Richard Alston and Matthew Bourne, who has produced commercially successful works using Tchaikovsky's music for his *Swan Lake* (1995) and Bizet's *Carmen* for his *The Car Man* (2000). These works normally fall into the category of direct correlation. Balanchine was concerned to achieve synthesis between music and dance, where the two media intermesh to form one statement. His works to the music of Stravinsky, with whom he had a long working relationship, include *Apollo* (1928), *Agon* (1957) and *Symphony in Three Movements* (1972). Mark Morris is consistently cited as an exceptionally musical dancer and choreographer; his musical choices are quite eclectic, ranging from such works as *Gloria* (1981) to Vivaldi, *Falling Down Stairs* (1997) to unaccompanied cello by Bach, Handel's *L'Allegro, il Penseroso ed il Moderato* (first produced in Brussels in 1988) and *Mozart Dances* (2006).

Interdependence is a term used for music and dance which happily coexist; for example in Bharata Natyam and many other Indian and African forms, there is a strong interrelationship between dancer and musician. This can be seen in the traditional telling of classical stories of much South Asian dance; in traditional and contemporary African dance, where the master drummer provides musical signals to the dancers (known as call and response); and also in flamenco with the *llamada* or 'call to the guitarist' by the dancer. In these cultural contexts, both musicians and dancers can improvise within a set framework.

Dances performed to a soundscape or sound environment fit into this category, where the dancers respond not to the rhythm, pulse or metre of the music, but to the environment or mood created by it. Nijinsky used this idea to great effect in *L'Après-midi d'un faune* (1912) where the dance responds not so much to Debussy's phrases and rhythms but rather to the atmosphere created by his music. Glen Tetley also used music atmospherically, as in

Pierrot Lunaire (1962), based on a Schoenberg *sprechstimme* piece, *Embrace Tiger and Return to Mountain* (1968) and *The Tempest* for the Ballet Rambert in 1979, with music by Arne Nordheim.

The third category, independence, refers to dance and music that have normally been composed separately, with or without prior consultation or association. This may mean that the two media are placed together only at the first performance, as was quite normal in the interrelationship of Cage sound scores with Cunningham's choreography, particularly for Events. As Cunningham defined the term, an 'Event' is a performance lasting about 90 minutes and consisting of bits and pieces from dances in the company's repertory. But instead of being presented as a set of obvious excerpts from longer works, these fragments are so intermingled as to constitute a new entity that is satisfying on its own terms. Meanwhile, the company's musicians Takehisa Kosugi, Michael Pugliese and David Tudor devised a score that usually combined electronic sounds with live sounds for violin, percussion and wind instruments and perhaps some recitations from essays.

STAGE FIVE: STRUCTURING AND FORMING THE DANCE

The overall structure of a dance is affected directly by questions such as:

Is this dance following the traditional, formal rules of composition, or a more alternative, experimental approach?

Does the dance rely on a narrative, with a specific beginning, middle and end, or does the choreographer 'cut and paste' sections in a more filmic way?

Is the music or accompaniment providing the form, as in theme and variation, verse and chorus, or is the music simply providing an environment, a landscape for the dance?

Can the choreographer piece together the various, already made sections of the dance in several different ways, as in thematic or episodic form?

Should the choreographer provide a recapitulation of salient aspects of the piece towards the end – some kind of coda or conclusion?

In the sections above, I have described fairly traditional, formal approaches to making choreography through the use of dance motifs and their development. But, I could also choose to create movement and then subject it to all kinds of painterly or filmic devices used currently, like layering, different forms of repetition, reversal, splicing, elaborating, juxtaposition, and collage and bricolage techniques that extend the choreographer's toolbox, even before we start to consider the possibilities provided by chance techniques or technology.

As in the other performing arts, dances can be constructed in a number of different ways. A five-act play, a three-act ballet, an oratorio, a symphony or a sonata each has specific demands as to its overall form. However, here we speak about structure at the macro level, where we consider the relationship of parts to the whole, the highlights and the climaxes, and yet form also plays its part in every small section at the micro-level. Each scene in a play, each movement in a sonata, and each section of a dance has its own internal and logical structure. Whether it is created by first year students making a solo based on Lady Macbeth for their first assessment, or an ensemble group making a non-literal piece, or Alwin Nikolais choreographing *Count Down*, the consideration of how to structure is still pertinent, though the methods applied might be radically distinct.

Here are some examples from professional choreographers:

• David Nixon is a Canadian choreographer who for the past 10 years has been Artistic Director of the Northern Ballet Theatre, based in Leeds, UK. Since the Company focuses on the theatricality and emotion of dramatic, narrative dance theatre, almost all Nixon's works have been narrative: titles such as *Romeo and Juliet*, *Madame Butterfly*, *Sleeping Beauty Tale*, *Hamlet* and *The Three Musketeers* have been created since 2001. Thus, the macro-structure is affected by the original play or novel, though Nixon usually works with a dramaturge and composer to develop the through-line, sub-plots and characters. For his new work, *Cleopatra* (2011), the music was written by Claude-Michel Schönberg (composer of the musical *Les Miserables*). As with many of his ballets, Nixon worked first on the relationships of the main characters in some research and development sessions, and much later involved the company as a whole in large ensembles and transitional sections. Thus, during the autumn of 2010 he explored (with dancers Martha Leebolt and Toby Batley as Cleopatra and Mark Antony) the intensely powerful and sexual relationship between these two protagonists in several pas de deux. Some recognizable dance motifs are depicted there which help to encapsulate the two strong characters and the relationship between them.

- Wayne McGregor, London-based choreographer of Random Dance and Choreographer in Residence at the Royal Opera House, revealed his approach to structuring dance when discussing the making of *The Millenarium* (1997). Typically, he starts a new project by generating content and exploring the kind of language he wants to develop in order to express the ideas (here, of how dance relates to new technologies and how technology might mediate ways of structuring content). Through setting tasks for his dancers based closely on the stimulus, he makes a phrase, develops a solo or duet, and then begins to see how the content might live in different ways. What would happen if the solo material was fused into a different sort of trio? What would happen if he retrograded or displaced the solo material, or placed it on the floor? Usually, a large number of phrases, solos, duets and ensemble sections are created in this way.

  After weeks of developing material, he then starts to structure, experimenting with accumulated patterns and rhythmic and spatial structures. Weeks are spent trying material in a range of combinations, observing, reconsidering and changing them: 'The content should continually resource the structure and vice versa, in a very lively dialogue' (Butterworth and Clarke, 1998: 107).

- Itamar Serussi Sahar (an Israeli choreographer working in The Netherlands) created *Phenomena* in 2009. First, he created and performed an individual solo work, *Cactus*, in which he explored his own physical movement language. In this solo, it was possible to see distinct 'sections' of material with slightly different stylistic qualities. Next, he investigated what he called 'experiential physicality' by translating this solo into a trio, danced by three female dancers, Genevieve Osborne-Horvàth,

Meri Pajunpää, and Orfée Schujt. The choreographer focused on two main issues in the research:

- communication with the dancers and understanding experientially the movement language in translation;
- the compositional aspect in the creative process.

In this process, the intention of the choreographer was to work individually with each dancer and push her beyond her accepted physical borders, and then to explore unfamiliar compositional territory to help break habitual methods of composing. The three dancers were fully involved in this creative process in which they became co-creators. The outcome was a fully embodied trio, where the dance language had been through such an intensive process that it no longer simply resembled the original solo; instead, the new solo, duet and trio material were structured so harmoniously into a stylistically coherent piece that no evidence of the previous distinct sections was visible.

STAGE SIX: COMPLETION/REHEARSAL

During the previous five stages of a compositional process, it is quite possible that at times choreographers lose sight of the journey's end. At certain points it might even feel as though the choreography has a mind of its own, or that the work is developing intuitively. The stages might not come consecutively, one after another; there might be slippage between them, as when you develop a phrase in many different ways, only to throw it away and start again. As McGregor, says, creativity often comes at the point where you make a mistake. Then you make another and another and another ... and at some point you suddenly make something original (FAR Programme, 2010).

How do you know when a dance is finished? Most choreographers work to a tight deadline which means that the première date has been set months beforehand. In the last week or so before the first night, aspects other than the choreography tend to take precedence; the music suddenly sounds different when played live by an orchestra or ensemble rather than the recording or rehearsal piano that the dancers have become familiar with; the set, or technology, or projections have to be figured out; and dancers struggle with new costumes rather than comfortable rehearsal gear. Often today professional companies plan to have some extra 'production time' where these elements can be synthesized; the lighting rig has to be erected and plotted, the designs made and rehearsed; the more complex and sophisticated the original intentions are, the more difficult they are to assemble. As choreographer/director, only when this part of the work is completed to your satisfaction can you evaluate the significance of what you have made. Your artistic creation may be reliant on the expertise of many other collaborators, and the integration and coherence of the whole have to be managed.

As a Dance Studies student, you will probably have to manage the same kinds of problems in miniature. The compositions that you make will be performed by you, or by a group of dancers whom you invite to work with you; they may be fellow students, with assessments of their own to manage. Essentially, you have to go through a dance-making process of your own, ensure the coherence of all the choreographic elements that you choose, and at the same time be prepared to rehearse the piece deeply so that your dancers have a clear understanding of the interpretation and are confident in performance (see Chapter 4, Performing dances).

STAGE SEVEN: EVALUATION/REFLECTION

The final step in the making of choreography in the university/college domain is the development of good practice in the evaluation of the three elements of planning, process and product – before, during and after any performance.

From my point of view as tutor and facilitator, a valuable lesson for students to learn after having made a piece of choreography is to critique their own work, having already captured the various processes of planning, creating, revising, rehearsing and producing in some kind of written form. These diaries, log books or portfolios document all the aspects of the creative process that you may very well forget but that would prove exceptionally useful for the next time you make a work. In addition, it is recommended that you develop your powers of reflection by writing a critical review of your own work. You may even be invited to present your practical research and critical findings of the work you have produced in some kind of viva voce or informal discussion with your tutor, in order to articulate and communicate your new understandings.

When you dance in a piece which has been choreographed by another member of the class, or when you work together in an ensemble, it is equally valuable to keep notes of your research findings and the way in which they might feed into the making of the piece. The ability to write on specific dance-making processes, to reflect on how they work for you, and to spend some time analysing those processes is really beneficial. Critically reviewing the work of others involves a consideration of differences in concept, context and methods. Students face a more difficult challenge when they work with professional choreographers; to be able to experience the process of making and performing the work, and afterwards to bring a critical eye to that engagement requires maturity, critical faculty and the ability to articulate opinions non-judgementally. I have therefore used the Critical Response Process developed by Liz Lerman with several different student groups.

The Critical Response Process is a set of guidelines for providing and receiving constructive criticism on choreography. It is a system that encourages viewing dance on a deeper level and the full articulation of observations and aesthetic choices. It can foster enthusiasm for problem-solving and decrease tension surrounding the giving and receiving of choreographic criticism. Each of the four steps is informed by respect, honesty and a genuine desire for the artist to create excellent work. The process depends upon (more or less) equal participation by the artist, a facilitator and an unspecified number of responders. It is seen as an evolving system that may be modified (Williams, 2002). The following steps are based on Williams's article published in the *Journal of Dance Education* (2002).

Step One: meaningful feedback

Responders are encouraged to express what has delighted, surprised, informed or moved them in the work presented. Each responder informs the artist of at least one thing about the work that has meaning for them, or 'brought them something special' (p. 94). The focus is on the work itself, and responders need to be specific in their comments, pointing to a particular moment, movement or place in the dance that they felt was significant. Step One provides opportunity for positive feedback to the artist and recognition of the work's merit.

Step Two: asking questions

In Step Two, the artist asks questions. A well-phrased question can promote insightful answers, so try to pose specific questions that have the potential to provoke layered answers. For example, rather than asking 'Did the ending work?', try to frame your questions so that responders can speak about the implied 'why' beneath the question.

Step Two foregrounds the artist's questions, and therefore the responders join the artist in consideration of the connections between intention and craft: how the artist's intentions find realization through choices of movement vocabulary, use of space, transitions, sound accompaniment or other choreographic elements.

Step Three: asking neutral questions

Step Three requires the responders to form their opinion into a neutral question. For example, rather than pronouncing that 'the costumes are ugly and ineffective', a neutral question might be 'What influenced your choice of the colour red for the costumes?' This method gives artists a chance to explore how their choices *read* to an audience. Neutral questions allow both the artist and the questioner an intellectual distance that is often useful: they open up dialogue and foster enthusiasm for problem-solving.

Step Four: expressing opinions

Step Four is the place for personal opinions, but the responder must ask the artist if s/he would like to hear an opinion about something specific (the costumes, the ending, the use of the stage space, etc.) and the artist can say yes or no. Artists are usually interested in hearing other people's perceptions. S/he can assimilate them or reject them – they are offered as opinion, and not choreographic fact. Sometimes 'fix-it' suggestions can be offered, as follows: 'I have an opinion about ____ and a suggestion. Do you want to hear it?'

The role of the facilitator

The facilitator may encourage the artist to summarize and restate what he or she heard at the end of each step of the process. By asking the artist to summarize responses and questions, the facilitator can point out important elements that have arisen.

The facilitator keeps the conversation relevant and focused, and decides when to move the discussion to the next step. S/he can assist both artist and responder to formulate questions, and can paraphrase the response for further clarification (www.danceexchange. org).

Since 2002, Liz Lerman has adapted and modified her approach to providing and receiving constructive criticism on choreography, and has offered many courses in America, Europe and elsewhere.

MAKING, APPRECIATING, COMMUNICATING

Finally, after having experienced the process of providing and receiving constructive criticism on choreography, students need to develop the skills of reflection and critical analysis of their own work and the work of others. The various stages of the choreographic process can be experienced individually, with peers, with professionals, and in applied contexts such as schools, community groups, site-specific performances and festivals, as demonstrated in Table 2.1.

During the three or four years of a Dance Studies programme, students will benefit from such a range of experiences, and be able to build on these skills and understandings in their choice of future career.

Table 2.1 Studying choreography in higher education

	Making	Performing	Appreciating	Communication of understandings
OWN	Own works Personal styles Developing personal strategies	Own works Personal (inner) intention Experiencing forms of communication	Conceptual processes Creative understandings Self-reflection	Log of dance-making process Critical review of own work Presentation of practical research
PEERS	Experiencing the work of peers Technical and conceptual challenges Shifts in group dynamic Differences in leadership approach	Performing the work of peers, leading to performance challenges which can be technical, conceptual or interpretative	Understanding concepts Cognitive understanding Reflection of meaning, style, interpretation Recognizing appropriateness of form to content	Writings on dance-making processes Analysing those processes Critical review of the work of others Consideration of differences in concept, context and methods Presentation of findings

continued

Table 2.1 continued

	Making	Performing	Appreciating	Communication of understandings
PROFESSIONALS	Experiencing the work of professionals: through learning repertoire; through experiencing the choreographic process with professionals Including differences in leadership approaches and in interrelationship within the group	Performing the work of choreographers Performing seminal, professional works through repertoire Performing professional works through working with artists in residence	Conceptual understanding Cognitive understanding Creative understanding of processes	Writings on dance-making processes Analysing those processes Critical review of professional choreography Consideration of differences in concept, context and methods Presentation of findings
APPLIED	Experiencing making work for applied contexts Intention Awareness of group needs	Experiencing a variety of performance intents, contexts and applications for dance-making Awareness of group needs	Appreciating the differences of intent Cognitive understandings of each process and context Appreciation of group needs	Writings on dance-making processes in applied contexts Analysing those processes Critical review of works made in applied contexts Consideration of differences in concept, context and methods Presentation of findings

FURTHER READING

Blom, L.A. and I.T. Chaplin (1982) *The Intimate Act of Choreography* Pittsburgh, Pa.: University of Pittsburgh Press

Blom, L.A. and I.T. Chaplin (1988) *The Moment of Movement: Dance Improvisation* London: Dance Books

Hawkins, A. (1991) *Moving from Within: A New Method for Dance making* New Jersey: a cappella

Humphrey, D. (1959, 1999) *The Art of Making Dances* New York: Random; second edition London: Dance Books

Minton, S.C. (1986, 1997) *Choreography: A Basic Approach Using Improvisation* Champaign, Ill.: Human Kinetics

Preston-Dunlop, V. (1998) *Looking at Dances: A Choreological Perspective on Choreography* London: Verve

Smith-Autard, J. (2010) *Dance Composition* sixth edition, London: Methuen Drama

Tuffnell, M. and C. Chrickmay (1990) *Body – Space – Image: Notes towards Improvisation* London: Dance Books

3

DANCE THEATRE HISTORY

This chapter provides a very brief, selective résumé of the history of ballet, modern dance, contemporary dance and new dance (sometimes called post-modern or independent dance) history. Of course, this subject is so huge that most readers will want to beg, steal or borrow more dance history books and explore the World Wide Web to supplement their knowledge. What has been attempted is a journey through chosen significant moments of theatre dance history, predominantly from the West, but referring to genres and styles from other continents and regions where possible. What becomes quite fascinating is how developments in theatre dance have occurred across times and spaces, across dates and cultures. The exciting thing about tracing some of the most significant recent periods in the history of dance is to realize the many links between one style and another, one country and another, affected by particular individuals.

I have drawn from many texts (see Further reading/research at the end of the chapter) for the sources of dominant ideas, and given examples of choreographic works that illuminate each period. But I have also chosen to focus particularly on the periods of dance history that I have lived through and experienced at first hand. However, I also offer a word of warning: as academic writers and as students we are reliant on:

- what has been documented;
- when and by whom;
- for what purpose;
- whose opinions they are.

There are many versions of the 'facts', none of them neutral, and there are many ways of tackling history:

> Almost everything we do carries a historical dimension – each step in the ballet class is imbued with centuries of tradition and change; each choreographic strategy rests on acceptance or rejection of others, whether formed years ago or yesterday. History is, therefore, woven into all our studies.
>
> (Carter 2004: 1)

The notion of acceptance/rejection can be perceived as a sort of pendulum swing: what one era proposes, another rejects. One decade follows another, detailing either evolution or revolution. As a student of Dance Studies, I hope you enjoy enhancing your knowledge of the past in order to help your understanding of the present. In this short journey you will travel only round Europe and criss-cross the Atlantic, touching on a few significant names. The vast dance cultures of Africa, India and China warrant their own texts, and then even more relationships can be identified.

BEGINNINGS OF DANCE DOCUMENTATION

Dance theatre history in the West is really only well documented from the French court ballets of the sixteenth and seventeenth centuries, but that does not mean that dance theatre performance did not exist prior to 1600. Chinese classical dance can also be traced back about 5,000 years to the royal court dances of the semi-divine culture of the Zhou, Tang and Song dynasties. Again, the character of the nation was expressed through dance; its movement was influenced by folk stories, classic myths and historic figures, and these dances expressed society's respect for morality, compassion, loyalty, wisdom and trustworthiness.

Dance as a sacred Hindu classical form was documented in 400 BC. The Natya Shastra (dance theory) of Bharata Muni provided the accepted theory of Indian classical dance in three categories: the spiritual dances performed in temples according to rituals were called Agata Nartanam; the intellectual form of dance performed in royal courts accompanied by classical music was named Carnatakam; and the dances of the commoners, Darbari Aatam, to educate them about religion, culture and social life, were danced in the courtyards of the temple precincts.

Both these forms incorporate strict technical training, precision and control; more importantly, the dancer's ability requires his spirituality to be reflected in the performance, as if the spirit was leading.

In the West, there is a tendency to begin our studies of performance by looking to Greece. Greek theatre practice is widely accepted to have originated in the Dithyramb, a song and dance performance celebrating the spring festival of Dionysus, at first wild and improvised, but later more elaborate, virtuosic and rehearsed. Amateurs became professional; performers developed their skills, and costumes helped to depict characters, but movement and gesture and their meaning and significance were at the heart of the development of dance.

In the West, there is also a long tradition of festivals and court entertainments which can be traced back at least to the processions and mummers' plays of the Middle Ages, which still had a religious function. Both France and Italy had engaged in entertainments for banquets or weddings, with music, costume, dancing and jousting. But from the 1570s, early court ballets became conscious inventions, an art form that fused all the arts. They tended to be secular events, frequently linking the desire for diversion and pleasure with some political motive. From contemporary drawings and paintings we can see that these ballets of the court were presented in large chambers with members of the court sitting on three sides; dance, poetry, music and design were the elements utilized to glorify the monarch and the state, underpinning the aristocratic perspective, and deliberately synthesizing entertainment, art and politics. Often, ballets derived from literary poetry or prose; symbolism and allegory were important components, and the performers could be nobles or professionals. Most court ballets ended with a ball in which all the spectators joined in the dancing.

EARLY BALLET IN EUROPE AND RUSSIA

The *Ballet comique de la Reine Louise* (1581) was created by Beaujoyeulx as a wedding festivity for the court; it was the first ballet to convey a unified dramatic plot, taken from an episode in Homer's

Odyssey. The specific characters of Circe, Minerva, Pan and Jupiter were developed symbolically; the enchantress Circe, who transformed men into animals, was defeated; since the ballet was meant to reconcile warring factions within France, the restoration of peace and goodwill at the end of the ballet represented the country's hopes for the future. 'This dramatic coherence marks the historic significance of the Ballet Comique, but it was the lavishness of its production that made it famous throughout Europe' (Cohen, 1992: 8).

In Italy and Sweden, England and particularly France, the *ballet de cour* (of the court) merged elements of figured social dances and music, classical plots with elaborate design and spectacle. In England, Ben Jonson and Inigo Jones emphasized drama; it was in France that the classical balletic tradition really developed, at first as a vehicle of the nobility. The most famous dancer of the period was Louis XIV:

> It is nearly dawn on the morning of 23 February 1653. So far, members of the French Royal court have been treated to an almost twelve-hour *mélange* of dancing, singing, poetry and elaborate stage effects depicting various scenes of village life, demonic activity and Greek myth. At the climax of Le Ballet Royal de la Nuit, and to herald the rising of the sun, the magnificently dressed King Louis XIV appears as *Le Roi Soleil* to lead the entire cast in a grand ballet.
>
> (Roebuck in Carter, 2004: 48–49)

Imagine Louis as Apollo, the sun god, surrounded by all his courtiers, and think about how dance as a discipline might have benefited from that monarchical interest. By 1661, a group of dancing masters had obtained permission from the king to form a professional organization, the Académie Royale de la Danse, whose aims were to improve the quality of dance instruction and establish scientific principles for the art. These ideas are the basis of our dance syllabi today.

The Italian-born dancer-composer Lully helped to transfer the ballet from court to theatre by setting up an all-male troupe of professional dancers at the Paris Opéra. Under the tutelage of Beauchamp, who is credited with codifying the existing ballet technique and developing systems for training, these dancers gained in facility and by 1681 female professional dancers joined the company. Feuillet and then Pécour contributed to this development, and by the early eighteenth century there was a permanent group of dancers at the Opéra, performing frequently in opera-ballets, and a school of dance had been officially decreed.

Early in the eighteenth century, ballet theoreticians proposed a type of dance that could stand on its own, fulfilling technical, expressive and narrative functions, called the *ballet d'action*. In the next century, there were developments in all aspects of the discipline; theory and practice were written and published, choreography explored the imitation of human actions and emotions, dancers became superb technicians able to express the dramatic and expressive possibilities of dance (see Au, 1988; Cohen, 1974, 1992).

Catherine the Great, Empress of Russia, was born in Germany and was married initially to the Russian tsar. During her reign, 1762–1796, within the context of her autocratic rule over Russia, she increased the control of landed gentry over serfs, and promoted education and the Enlightenment among the elite, introducing ideas to modernize and civilize Russia. Fortunately for the development of dance, she also engaged ballet masters from Western Europe to arrange spectacles and festivities for her court; established choreographers from France (Didelot, Perrot and Saint-Léon) and dancers of the calibre of Marie Taglioni and Fanny Elssler came to create and perform.

Just a century later, the Mariinsky Theatre in St Petersburg and the Bolshoi Theatre in Moscow became state-owned, with ballet companies and training schools producing skilled, virtuoso dancers. The Frenchman Marius Petipa is generally agreed to have been the most influential ballet master and choreographer working there. Originally employed as a dancer, then assistant choreographer at the Imperial Ballet in St Petersburg, he assumed the post of chief choreographer, creating a repertoire of original works for the Imperial Ballet. From 1871 to 1903 he created over 50 ballets, and revived a number of works by other ballet masters, the most famous being *La Bayadère* (1877), *The Sleeping Beauty* (1890) and *Swan Lake* (with Ivanov, 1895).

Petipa was often inspired by the technical capabilities or distinctive characteristics of specific ballerinas such as Carlotta Brianza and

Virginia Zucchi, two dramatic dancers from Italy. At that time the standard pas de deux consisted of an adagio for the couple, a variation for each and a technically brilliant coda, often consisting of grands jetés (big jumps) for the male dancer, and fast turns on pointe for the ballerina. We still see these today in traditional ballets. Another Italian, Pierrina Legnani, was famous for her whipped turns (fouettés) which the Russian ballerinas soon mastered, and which we still see danced by Odile, the Black Swan in Act 3 of *Swan Lake*. Petipa brought to classical choreography technical invention and a sense of restrained elegance and feeling.

In the history of dance we can trace both revolutionary and evolutionary ideas: for example, Michel Fokine was the next major Russian choreographer, who tried to challenge the set conventions and codes of the Imperial Ballet, and who converted the classical vocabulary to more dramatic ends thanks to the opportunities presented by Diaghilev.

DIAGHILEV AND THE BALLETS RUSSES

In 1909, Serge Diaghilev, a Russian impresario, formed a company of Russian dancers to play a season of ballet in Paris. The Ballets Russes, as they became known, astounded Parisian audiences with their technical prowess, their dramatic and glamorous presentations and most of all with their exoticism. Diaghilev brought together talented artists – dancers, choreographers, composers, designers – with bold, imaginative vision, and ensured that story, music, dance and design were closely integrated. In the first seasons, a self-consciously Russian element dominated the productions: Russian folk tales inspired these ballets, and many of them were designed by the Russian-born artist Léon Bakst, whose brilliant colours, Art Nouveau elements and sense of the erotic helped to communicate a sense of ballet as a total work of art, a spectacle.

The Ballets Russes' first choreographer was Michel Fokine, who not only presented his poetic *Les Sylphides* (1909) but collaborated with Igor Stravinsky to produce *The Firebird* (1910), followed by *Petrouchka* (1911) which was inspired by the puppets of Russian fairs. Fokine delighted in subverting the classical turnout in this ballet – the introverted Petrouchka, danced by Nijinsky, moves with his feet turned in and his body painfully tense and closed. This company seemed to revolutionize the arts of Europe in the early twentieth century; the dancers were highly trained, expressive and confident; the artistic collaborators were willing to take risks and enjoy the political and artistic freedom of the West, and in particular Paris, the centre of much artistic revolution.

Diaghilev's company thrived in Europe, and soon established itself permanently, allowing him to pursue the ambition of employing great artists to create entirely new ballets each season. Despite the success of Fokine's work, he encouraged Nijinsky, a male dancer of great virtuosity and charisma, to begin creating choreographies such as *L'Après-midi d'un faune* (1912) and *The Rite of Spring* (1913).

In 1912, the sexual nuances and startling angularity of Nijinsky's movement in *Faune* to Debussy's tone poem provoked intense reactions among the audience; in many senses the relationship of faun and nymphs provided an erotic fantasy which shocked the spectators of the day. His next work, *Le Sacre du printemps* (*The Rite of Spring*), was even more difficult to comprehend, exploring as it does the primitive rituals of a rural Russian community believing in the sacrifice of a chosen maiden for the good of the community. In style, this work was far removed from the balletic concept of flow and beauty, as again Nijinsky abandoned academic ballet technique in favour of primeval walking, stamping and jumping. Stravinsky's score was both dissonant and rhythmically complex, Roerich's scenography harsh and primitive, and essentially (as we have subsequently realized) this ballet marks the true beginnings of modernism in the art form. As is well documented, the audience did not understand these intentions and reacted violently to the première, though no doubt Diaghilev was pleased with the publicity.

During the years of the First World War, Diaghilev sought new collaborators among the avant-garde artists working in Paris; Nijinsky was dismissed from the company following his marriage during a tour to South America, and later suffered from schizophrenia. Léonard Massine emerged as the new choreographic talent. His ballet *Parade* (1917), as conceived by the artist Cocteau, was composed to music by Satie with sets by Picasso. Two dancers wore huge Cubist sculptures, two were in a horse costume, there were acrobats, a conjuror who breathes fire – a far cry from the romanticism of the previous century, and all this demonstrated a new chic, modernist era for the Ballets Russes. Other popular Massine ballets were *La Boutique fantasque* (1919) based on a fairy tale of dolls that come to life, and *The Three-Cornered Hat* (1919) featuring Spanish dancing and a mock bullfight.

The First World War saw the collapse of the Russian, German, Austro-Hungarian and Ottoman empires; Russia came under Communist control after the Revolution in 1917, and Diaghilev never returned to his country. By 1920, the Ballets Russes' ballets depicted European topical interests such as beach culture, films and sport with such works as *Jeux* (1913, Nijinsky with music by Debussy) and *Les Biches* (1924, Bronislava Nijinska with music by Poulenc). French modernist artists such as Matisse, Braque and Derain were the new designers, while the choreographers Léonide Massine, Nijinska and Balanchine approached the creation of new ballets in various innovative ways. On Diaghilev's death in 1929, the company disbanded and individuals scattered across Western Europe and beyond; yet, as we will see later in the chapter, his influence continued and countries worldwide benefited from the knowledge and skills the Ballets Russes had developed in just 20 years.

THE EARLY DEVELOPMENT OF THE AMERICAN DANCE FORM: FROM ISADORA

Meanwhile, three American women, Loie Fuller (1862–1928), Isadora Duncan (1877–1927) and Ruth St Denis (1879–1968), are credited with making the first steps towards a new form of dancing in the USA, dance that was beyond extravaganza and entertainment, or merely repetition of what was happening in Europe, but dance which would be considered more artistically fulfilling. Individually, they approached this goal in different ways.

Loie Fuller created a style of dance which was characterized by its visual effects, focusing on stage lights and colours on her long skirts or draperies, representing natural elements or objects – fire, the sea, a butterfly, etc. She had little dance training, but was interested in scientific developments leading to new aspects of stage technology, electric lighting, coloured gels, slide projections, etc. In 1892 she accepted a contract with the Folies Bergère in Paris, where her work related well to the fashionable Art Nouveau style;

her dancing appealed to many Symbolist painters and poets. For *Fire Dance* (1895) she invented underlighting: she stood on a pane of frosted glass illuminated from underneath, and danced to Wagner's *Ride of the Valkyries*. Always open to new inventions, she devised ambitious themes with an all-female company to increasingly progressive music; at the Paris Exposition in 1900 she had her own theatre where she presented her choreographies. Her compatriots Duncan and St Denis were both knowledgeable about her work, though their own journeys were quite different.

Isadora Duncan is now remembered as much as a symbol of emancipation from the traditional roles of wife and mother and for her sexual freedom as for her dancing. She advocated naturalness in her movement style and themes of universal emotions, aspirations and inner impulses. She often danced solo on a stage with a plain backdrop, to a single piano, wearing a Greek tunic with bare feet, inspired by her fascination for ancient Greece. When she and her family moved to London in 1899, she met critics and artists who encouraged her to use great works of art as stimuli for her dances. Convinced that movement should spring from within, that dance was an expression of personal emotion rather than representation, she was extremely influential. She inspired a great many artists, writers and sculptors, and indeed wrote a number of books about her philosophy of life. She performed all over Europe and in Russia where in 1904 she was seen by Fokine, Diaghilev and other members of Russia's dance world. Returning to America in 1908 for a visit and tour, she danced triumphantly at the Metropolitan Opera House in New York.

Back in Europe, she set up a school in Germany and continued to tour her solo performances. She had two children out of wedlock, one with Edward Gordon Craig, the stage designer, and a second with Paris Singer, but both children were drowned in 1913 in a car accident in Paris. During the First World War she made dances that portrayed sombre emotions and resilience in the face of adversity: *La Marseillaise* (1915) and the *Marche slave* (1916) were both perceived as dances of social protest, implicitly referring to the French Revolution and the Russian uprising. Indeed, she lived in Russia for at least two years, supporting the Communist regime. Ever the idealist, she continued to dance and teach, but her later life continued to be both self-indulgent and tragic.

The third compatriot, Ruth St Denis, had much more influence on American dance through her union with Ted Shawn. She began her career in acrobatics and skirt dancing, studied ballet and Spanish dance, and created many 'oriental' dances which made no pretence at authenticity. Her first major dance *Radha* (1906) was an exotic representation of Hindu temple dancing, and *The Nautch* in 1908 evoked Indian street dancers in pseudo-Kathak style – rhythmic stamping, whirling and sinuous arm gestures. She created a full-length Egyptian work with a cast of 50 dancers and musicians led by St Denis in several roles.

In 1914 her meeting with Ted Shawn, who became both her husband and her partner, was to be a significant factor in the development of American modern dance. Together they established the school Denishawn in Los Angeles which offered a wide variety of dance styles in the curriculum, including dance history and philosophy, in the attempt to engage body, mind and spirit. Both St Denis and Shawn taught, choreographed and performed in their Denishawn company; under Shawn's influence, the repertoire expanded to include many other dance cultures such as Amerindian, North African and Spanish elements. They both became interested in music visualization – trying to reflect the structure of a piece of music without the imposition of story or the interpretation of emotions. Notably, in addition to the first all-male dances choreographed by Shawn, the company toured numerous times during the 1910s and 1920s, including a tour to Asia, which was to prove very stimulating. Significantly, company members included Martha Graham and Charles Weidman, followed by Doris Humphrey, three of the next generation of American modern dance choreographers. By providing training and performance experience in various dance forms other than ballet, and by treating the dance as art rather than mere entertainment, they clearly influenced the next generation.

DANCE EXPRESSIONISM IN GERMANY/EUROPE

Another, quite different, dance revolution had been taking place in Europe during this period, based in Germany and Switzerland and initiated by Rudolf Laban (1879–1958). Laban is now best remembered for his work on dance analysis and notation, but his ideas about the art of movement permeate many other fields such as recreational dance, education and therapy. Early on, from 1899 to 1914, he was attracted to all kinds of art and performance and made explorations in visual arts, dance and movement in Budapest, Munich and Paris. Living at a time when the arts, sciences, psychology and social theories were developing and interrelating, he experienced aspects of Art Nouveau, the body-culture approaches of Rudolf Bode and Emile Jaques-Dalcroze, café society and cabaret. He worked as a pageant director in Munich, studied drawing and architecture in Paris, was influenced by Kandinsky and Klee of the Blaue Reiter group and the atonal music of Schoenberg. After all these experiences he was ready to begin teaching, leading and guiding others. At an experimental communal summer school in Ascona, Switzerland, artists from various art forms came together, ready to participate in creating new forms of dance. Laban devised 'Movement choirs', involving improvisation, musical theory and structures from visual design, and developed concepts about dance, sound and word (*Tanz, Ton, Wort*). Mary Wigman (1886–1973) was a student and colleague from this period.

When the First World War broke out he went to Zurich, working on his movement principles and notation system, and contributing dances to Dadaist cabarets. Later, he published many books about his philosophy of the art of dance, choreographed professionally for opera and theatre, continued to work on movement choirs and developed schools and training programmes, where Kurt Jooss (1901–1979) became a student. During the 1920s, Laban was directing both professional chamber groups performing theatrical works, often based on social commentary, and amateur movement choirs in many towns all over Germany. In 1930 he accepted the post of Ballet Master at the Berlin State Opera, though many dancers took exception to his ideas, and he was increasingly aware of the rise of fascism. His research, however, continued and his *Ein Leben für den Tanz (A Life for Dance)* was published in 1935. He fled Germany in 1936 after the Nazi party banned his performance of *Tauwind* (a huge movement choir) in the week of the Berlin Olympics. His work continued in England where until his death he was immersed in applying his movement theories to creative dance in the school curriculum as Modern Educational Dance (see Chapter Six below).

Mary Wigman was an innovator of what became known as *Ausdruckstanz*, German Expressionistic dance, in the mid-1920s and 1930s. She first studied eurhythmics with Dalcroze at his school in Hellerau, then worked with Rudolf Laban on movement studies. When she first met him at a summer school near Ascona, Switzerland, in summer 1913, Laban was already a painter and designer, and his vision was for a new work of art, a combination of dance, music and poetry, which led him to try to develop a form of movement very different from the ballet of the period. His new movement system was based on natural organic movement of the human body and the principles of tension and relaxation, incorporating first a form of gymnastic training, then improvisation, simple solo dances and group sketches. Laban worked with drum in hand, inventing and experimenting; his students danced with music and without it, with words, phrases, poetry; their experiments may not have led to a definite artistic form but Wigman later wrote: 'Laban had the extraordinary quality of setting you free artistically, enabling to find your own roots, and thus stabilized, to discover your own potentialities, to develop your own technique and your individual style of dancing' (Wigman, 1984: 35).

Wigman's choreographic career started with *Witch Dance* (1914), executed in silence, wearing a mask; most of her works were solos, sombre, emotionally intense and often concerned with man and his fate. In her later dances she confronted issues such as memorializing those who died in war, as in *Totenmal* (1930), or the inevitability of old age *(Song of Fate*, 1935). Her work is often associated with the German Expressionist painters, with use of distortion and exaggeration. Her school in Dresden began in 1920, educating many important modern dancers including Hanya Holm, Harald Kreutzberg and Gret Palucca. She and her company toured the USA three times between 1930 and 1933 and she was so well received that Holm was sent to open a Wigman school in New York. During the Second World War, Wigman remained in Germany but her activities were curtailed by the Nazis. She resumed her work after the war, first in Leipzig and then West Berlin.

Another Laban student, Kurt Jooss, became a teacher and choreographer (at the Folkwangschuhle in Essen) where in 1928 he founded a group that began the Kurt Jooss Company, devising a choreographic style that blended modern expressive dance with classical ballet technique without pointe shoes. He is most famous for his 1932 work *The Green Table*, a protest against the futility of war, with scenes which ridicule the diplomats of the period and feature the figure of Death (originally danced by Jooss) who gradually dominates his victims: soldier, old woman, young girl, resistance fighter. The juxtaposition of war cabinet decision-making and human tragedy is still poignant and pertinent today. Jooss won a choreographic competition in Paris with this piece, but his explicit criticism of the Nazis meant that he and his company were forced to leave Germany the following year.

BALLET IN THE UK

England benefited hugely from the body of knowledge accrued under Diaghilev, as did North and South America, when the company disbanded. Both Marie Rambert and Ninette de Valois had experienced working with the Ballets Russes; Rambert established the Rambert School of Ballet and a small company in London in the 1920s, and in 1926 de Valois opened the London Academy of Choreographic Art. Both, in distinct ways, contributed to the growth of British ballet, as did the contributions of Markova and Dolin, and of the Camargo Society.

Prior to 1920, Britain's dance teaching and performance tradition were reliant predominantly on the influence of a broad spectrum of foreign teachers and performers, and particularly on the style of Russian ballet brought to Europe by the Ballets Russes. Before the 1930s four main methods of classical ballet training had been introduced in London. In 1920, the original committee of the Association of Operatic Dancing, renamed the Royal Academy of Dance in 1935, represented the classical ballet schools and methods of Italy, France, Denmark and Russia. Eduard Espinosa from the tradition of the Paris Opéra had taught in London from 1896, and the Italian Enrico Cecchetti from 1918 to 1923, two individuals who would prove to be influential on the development of British ballet. Adeline Genée, a ballerina from the Danish Royal Ballet, performed in London regularly in the first decade of the century, and Nicholas Legat opened a school specializing in Russian classical ballet in 1923.

Rambert and de Valois initiated the drive to establish a British ballet scene and environment comparable to others in Europe. Dance technique was provided by and developed from these French, Italian, Danish and Russian schools and styles proliferating in London. Specifically, the work of five choreographers, Fokine, Nijinska, Massine, Balanchine and Jooss, were well known through performances in London by the Ballets Russes, Ballets 1933 and Ballets Jooss.

The British tradition of the 1930s tended to consider ballet as an aspect of narrative. Choreographers such as de Valois, Antony Tudor and Frederick Ashton each found a language that was expressive and that told a story or evoked mood, character and situation in dance terms. Together, de Valois and Ashton laid the foundations for what would become the Royal Ballet; unlike the Ballets Russes, the English company was not innovative, but concentrated on meticulous execution, a lyrical elegance and strong musicality that became a distinctive style. Characterization and a fusion of dance, music and scenography are evident in de Valois's new ballets: *Job* (1931), *The Haunted Ballroom* (1934), *The Rake's Progress* (1935), *The God's Go A-Begging* (1936), *Checkmate* (1937) and *The Prospect before Us* (1940). Frederick Ashton was also a prolific choreographer who was able to provide works that could make up a well-balanced programme, creating ballets that

> by their technical and interpretive demands, helped to turn young dancers into virtuosi, even into artists, and they formed the basis of what has come to be recognised as the English style of classical ballet, a style expressive of what we like to think of as the English national character – lyrical, precise, well-mannered, yet robust – but flavoured by Latin and Gallic elements in Ashton's own temperament and background, a certain chic, a certain flamboyance, which counteracted any tendency towards gentility or dowdiness.
>
> (Vaughan in Jordan and Grau, 1996: 1–2)

For example, between 1935 and 1940 he created for the Sadler's Wells company several new works including *Le Baiser de la fée* (1935), *Apparitions* (1936), *Les Patineurs* (1937), *Wedding Bouquet* (1938), *Horoscope* (1938), *Judgement of Paris* (1938) and *Dante Sonata*

(1940). But the British public were also interested in seeing revivals of the great Russian works like *Sleeping Beauty* and *Swan Lake*. Antony Tudor, meanwhile, remained with the Ballet Rambert where he created *Jardin aux lilas* (1936) and *Dark Elegies* (1937), before travelling to America in 1940 to help establish the American Ballet Theatre.

British ballet continues to thrive with five major companies: the Royal Ballet, its sister company Birmingham Royal Ballet (BRB), English National Ballet, Northern Ballet and Scottish Ballet. The Royal Ballet's artistic directors have included Kenneth MacMillan (www.kennethmacmillan.com), who produced 60 ballets in his lifetime, John Field, Antony Dowell and Monica Mason. MacMillan was best known for his long three act dramatic story works that explored the human psyche – *Romeo and Juliet* (1965), first danced by Fonteyn and Nureyev, *Manon* (1974), *Mayerling* (1978) and *The Judas Tree* (1992), his last ballet. The Ballet Rambert, meanwhile, changed its name and mission under Richard Alston in 1987 and as the Rambert Dance Company has developed as a contemporary company under Christopher Bruce and Mark Baldwin (www. rambert.org.uk; their history continues later in the chapter).

BALLET IN AMERICA

In the USA of the early 1920s, interest in ballet tended to be minimal, as it was considered a European art form unrelated to the American culture. But in 1933, after a tour by the Ballet Russe de Monte Carlo, with Massine as choreographer, Alexandra Danilova and a set of Russian émigré 'baby ballerinas', Lincoln Kirstein invited George Balanchine to New York to establish a school and a small company, American Ballet.

George Balanchine was born in St Petersburg in 1904, entered the Imperial School of Theatre and Ballet, and appeared on the stage of the Mariinsky Theatre as a student dancer in *The Sleeping Beauty*. Though his studies were interrupted by the Bolshevik Revolution, in 1918 he resumed his training, graduated and was accepted into the Mariinsky company. Though the school had given him intimate knowledge of the classical vocabulary, he was not interested in imitating the style of older productions and his methods of extending and modifying tradition became more experimental. In 1924 he left Russia with the Soviet State Dancers and decided to stay in Western Europe, joining Diaghilev's Ballets Russes as soloist and resident choreographer. During five years he learned much from dancing the work of Fokine, Massine and Nijinska; whereas Petipa had framed his principal dancers with fairly static settings of groups and formations, Fokine made members of the corps de ballet an active ensemble, reshaping it in response to the movements of the principals and contributing in an active way. Balanchine developed this idea one stage further: 'the brilliant handling of groups of dancers was to emerge as one of the dominant traits of Balanchine's style' (McDonagh, 1983: 46).

Balanchine was an expressive force and Diaghilev was able to guide and challenge him, assigning him scores like Stravinsky's *The Song of the Nightingale* and Reita's *Barabau*. In 1928 he choreographed his first major ballet, *Apollon musagète*. Stylistically, this work was seen as contemporary classicism (or neo-classicism), which remained a favoured style. His last ballet for the Ballets Russes was to Prokofiev's score *The Prodigal Son* (1929) with primitive scenery and costumes designed by Rouault, an opportunity for imaginative invention and daring sexuality.

As you will remember, Diaghilev's death in 1929 led to the demise of the company and the dancers scattered all over the world. Balanchine met Lincoln Kirstein in London in 1933, and was invited to instigate a school and company in the USA. Balanchine's works here tended to be in the neo-classical style, musically and technically based but without spectacle: his first, made with students, was *Serenade* (1935), which he conceived without libretto to *Tchaikovsky's Serenade in C for String Orchestra*, his first new ballet for American dancers (McDonagh, 1983: 58). But he also successfully choreographed the first of 18 Broadway musicals and revues, including *On Your Toes* (1936). After the Second World War Kirstein formed Ballet Society with Balanchine as Artistic Director and the company moved to New York City Center (later to the Lincoln Center) and was renamed New York City Ballet (NYCB).

Balanchine's ballets here were characterized by the abandonment of conventional, emotionally involving story ballets in favour of abstraction driven by the logic of the chosen musical score. Music and its interpretation lie at the heart of most of his ballets, and it is no surprise that he was a trained musician or that his father and brother were composers. The titles of many of his ballets derive from the names of musical compositions or composers, e.g. *Symphony in C* (1948, by Bizet); *Ivesiana* (1954, to music by Charles Ives); *Stars and Stripes* (1958 to Sousa), and *Vienna Waltzes* (1977). His long-term relationship with his fellow countryman was celebrated in the Stravinsky Festival in 1972, in personal tribute to him, with *Symphony in Three Movements*, *Violin Concerto* and *Duo Concertant*.

Balanchine's personal aesthetic is characterized by what has become termed neo-classicism. His legacy is the plotless ballet, soundly grounded in technique, musically based, without story or character content, needing no references to dramatic action, although he did of course produce full-length, more dramatic works like *The Nutcracker* (1954) and *Don Quixote* (1965). He was joined at NYCB by Jerome Robbins who had danced in many of Balanchine's works for Broadway and had choreographed many more himself: during the 1950s, barely a year went by without a new Robbins ballet and a new Robbins musical. With Balanchine, he choreographed *Jones Beach* in 1950, and directed and choreographed Irving Berlin's *Call Me Madam*, starring Ethel Merman.

In 1951, Robbins created the now celebrated dance sequences in Rodgers and Hammerstein's *The King and I*; his major musicals include *The Pajama Game* (1954), *Bells Are Ringing* (1956) with Bob Fosse, and in 1957 he conceived, choreographed and directed a show that some feel is his crowning achievement: *West Side Story*. His works for NYCB include the non-narrative, classically based *Dances at a Gathering* (1969) and *Goldberg Variations* (1971).

Through the decade 1960–1970, Balanchine and Robbins at NYCB were working in the same city as Antony Tudor (American Ballet Theatre), the early modern dance choreographers Martha Graham, Doris Humphrey and José Limón, the African Americans Alvin Ailey and Arthur Mitchell (Dance Theatre of Harlem), and the innovative post-moderns, led by Merce Cunningham, among many others. Imagine the possibilities for fruitful influence, exchange and collaboration.

MARTHA GRAHAM AND MODERN DANCE

Martha Graham was an extraordinary performer, a choreographer of outstanding originality and the creator of a systematic dance technique. She pioneered many of the teaching methods now considered the norm in modern dance education: the use of both parallel and turnout, contraction and release, floor work, spirals, fall and recovery. As she created new dances, new vocabulary was also introduced: leaps with the body leaning forward in contraction, as in *Primitive Mysteries* (1931); triplets crossing the floor, percussive movement, cupped hands and angular arms, large circular leg gestures in *Cave of the Heart* (1946) and *Diversion of Angels* (1948).

She made her choreographic debut in New York in 1926 with a programme of her own devising including lyrical and pictorial dances that barely demonstrated the Graham to come. She continued to experiment with the architecture of the body and the function of each joint in order to discover the freedom of movement that was available to her. She also explored themes that spoke of her passions in dances like *Revolt* (1927) and *Heretic* (1929). She experienced a richly creative period between 1928 and 1938, when her group dances expressed the need to reaffirm rituals in human lives: *Two Primitive Canticles, Primitive Mysteries* (1931) and *Ceremonials*. Her solos tended to distil the universal, timeless human experience in such works as *Lamentation* (1930) and *Frontier* (1935). In *Lamentation*, a shrouded figure sits contracted in agony, pulling, twisting and reaching, expressing in physical form inner feelings that any one watching could apply to his or her own experiences. Graham wrote that she wore a long tube of material to indicate 'the tragedy that obsesses the body, the ability to stretch inside your own skin, to witness and test the boundaries of grief.' (1991: 117). The stimuli for *Frontier* included not only the notion of physical frontiers as experienced by early Americans, but the passage from the known, the safe, to the unsafe unknown, perhaps a release of the spirit. These two seminal works provide a heritage for the young dancer, of meaningful themes physicalized in a revolutionary way.

Many other American themes abound in her works: throughout the 1940s, she produced large group choreographies distilling ideas of goodness and evil, such as *American Document* (1938), *Letter to the World* (1940) and *Appalachian Spring* (1944). Other works that reflected her interest in mythical characters from classical Greek sources include *Cave of the Heart* (1946) on the legend of Medea; *Errant into the Maze* (1947), derived from the story of the labyrinth and the Minotaur; *Night Journey* (1947), presenting Jocasta when she is about to kill herself; *Clytemnestra* (1958); and *Phaedra* (1962). Essentially these dances tended to present themes from an unmistakable American perspective, and most were created with Graham herself in the central, often matriarchal role.

Graham's legacy was embodied in her choreographic masterworks and her invention of a new and codified dance language. The Graham technique became the first enduring alternative to the idiom of classical ballet. Powerful, dynamic, jagged and filled with tension, this vocabulary, combined with Graham's distinctive system of training, establishes her as a true dance innovator. In addition, she danced for more than 60 years, was a passionate and articulate speaker, a creative artist and an independent spirit.

Graham's compatriots in the early modern dance included Doris Humphrey, Charles Weidman and José Limón. Humphrey's choreography explored the nuances of the human body's responses to gravity, embodied in her principle of fall and recovery (see Chapter 2 above). Her choreography from these early years includes *Water Study* (1928), *Life of the Bee* (1929), *Two Ecstatic Themes* (1931) and *The Shakers* (1931).

The Humphrey–Weidman Company was successful even during the Great Depression, touring America and developing new styles and new works based on current events and concerns. In the mid-1930s, Humphrey created the New Dance Trilogy, a triptych comprising *With My Red Fires* (1935), *New Dance* (1935) and the now lost *Theater Piece* (1935; see a description in Cohen, 1974). Her works tended to be less intense than Graham's, working in both symphonic and dramatic form, but she still engaged with the lives of twentieth-century Americans. Her book *The Art of Making Dances* was published posthumously in 1959 (see Chapter 2 above).

From the companies of Humphrey-Weidman and Graham we can trace young choreographers who either evolved these early modern dance forms or revolted against them. José Limón continued the Humphrey traditions, particularly in terms of the dramatic, and is best known for *The Moor's Pavane* (1949), which is based on the relationships of the four principal characters of Shakespeare's *Othello*, and *Missa Brevis* (1958). His was the first American dance company to perform in Paris in 1950. Anna Sokolow and Merce Cunningham had both danced with Graham and yet both rejected narrative structures in their own works; many dance-makers of this generation felt that dramatic content was not necessary, and even that expressivity limited movement invention in some way.

MERCE CUNNINGHAM

Cunningham may not have been the first choreographer to dispense with story-telling and emotion, but he was certainly the first to treat music and dance as distinct and wholly independent activities that simply occur in a common time and place. This dissociation dates from the beginning of his professional work with John Cage, who had evolved a method of composing music based on structure using units of time: 'From the start of their association, Cage and Cunningham have simply agreed on a certain time structure – for example, eight parts of two minutes each – and then gone off independently to compose the music and the dance' (Tomkins, 1968: 244).

Another shared influence was the notion of creating barriers to composers' or choreographers' aesthetic personal tastes by using *aleatory* or chance techniques. Going beyond individual self-expression, Cage proposed a kind of purposeless play, eliminating all control and turning composition over to chance. Many writers, painters and composers have also used these ideas of indeterminacy, but none so purely as Cage, who felt that traditional attitudes to art – communicating ideas and emotions, organizing meaningful patterns, realizing universal truths – were obsolete. A typical method of composition was to refer to the *I Ching*, or *Book of Changes*, an ancient Chinese book of charts and hexagrams used for obtaining oracles according to the tossing of coins or sticks. Whereas Cage allowed these operations to dictate whole music compositions, Cunningham regarded chance as a practical tool to make his dances richer and more interesting while still relying on his own powers of conscious invention, his memory and his personal taste.

Cunningham began his dance career with Bonnie Bird in Seattle in the 1930s, attended the summer programme at Bennington in 1939, and joined the Graham company as a soloist soon after. His personal style was in direct contrast to Graham's strength, weight and expressive power; his natural gifts were those of lightness, elevation and incredible speed. While touring with the company, he also took ballet lessons at the School of American Ballet, where

Balanchine was director. When he started making solo work, Edward Denby wrote of him: 'I have never seen a first recital that combined such impeccable taste, intellectually and decoratively, such originality of dance material, and so sure a manner of presentation' (Denby in Tomkins, 1968: 256).

Cunningham started to teach and to make dances with his students who had received their fundamental training elsewhere. Their physical and intellectual capacities did not always satisfy his requirements, however, and in the early 1950s he began to form a company of pupils who had come to him with little or no previous training. He developed a technique based on his own body where the articulation of the back and torso is highly developed, with the central point of balance in the lower region of the spine. The spine can turn on its own axis or project into space in different directions, acting as a source of initiation for the arms and legs. He evidently took the dexterity of the legs learned from ballet but transformed it spatially (see Chapter 1 above).

Cunningham's choreography was equally esoteric; although his dance language was performed by technically skilled dancers, he was simply interested in composing human movement in space and time without any external referent. His use of space upturned the usual stage concept; every part of the performance space was considered as important as centre stage, and often several duets or trios would take place in different locations, often sharing the space with art-works created by like-minded artists such as Robert Rauschenberg and Jasper Johns, both of whom worked with the company as Artistic Advisors. The meaning of the dance was usually left open, audiences were encouraged to respond individually to what they viewed, even where they viewed, and there were often many centres of activity on stage at any one time. Equally, his choreography was not governed by traditional concepts of form, or by the logical progression of movements building towards a climax. In *Field Dances* (1963) each dancer has a simple series of movements; they could enter or exit the stage at will, and perform the movements in any order and any number of times. In 1964 he initiated *Events*, which allowed him to recycle material from other works, in various orders, in various performance spaces such as galleries or gymnasia, parks or squares. Often the dancers did not know what sections of works were to be performed until they read the lists back stage.

Cunningham began investigating dance on film in the 1970s, and after 1991 choreographed using the computer program Life Forms, now called DanceForms. He is also well known for his filmdances, like *Square Game* (1976) or *Locale* (1979), co-directed with Charles Atlas, or *Points in Space* (1986) and the film *Beach Birds for Camera* (1992) co-directed with Eliot Caplan. In 1998 Cunningham explored motion capture technology with digital artists Paul Kaiser and Shelley Eshkar to create *Hand-drawn Spaces*, a three-screen animation, and this led to a live dance for the stage, *BIPED* (1999), for which Kaiser and Eshkar provided the projected decor.

Cunningham died in 2010, but he has left a remarkable legacy: not only all the current contemporary choreographers who were influenced by his philosophy, technique, his methods of generating dance content or his structural strategies, but also the way in which he planned for a final, two-year Legacy Tour and the preservation of his oeuvre in digital form by creating dynamic 'Dance Capsules' that document his legacy for future generations and allow ongoing study and enjoyment of his work.

CONTEMPORARY DANCE IN THE UK

In 1966, influenced by his visit to the USA and by the integrated classical and contemporary forms of Nederlands Dans Theater (NDT), Norman Morrice, Artistic Director of the Ballet Rambert, decided that the Rambert Company should extend its classical background by studying modern dance and bringing in choreographers from America (Percival, 1980: 73). In 1967, four Glen Tetley works were taken into the repertoire and Tetley came to work in London. Alternating daily classes in contemporary and classical ballet technique for the first time, the dancers found 'excitement in the old technique just by virtue of the contrast with the new one' (Percival, 1971: 142). The need for such technical mastery was stimulated by works like Tetley's *Pierrot Lunaire* (1962), remounted on the Rambert Company in 1967. The piece used an eclectic dance language to illustrate an allusive and complex style based on *commedia dell'arte* characters. Tetley's idiosyncratic and highly personalized vocabulary and choreographic style no doubt grew in part from his eclectic background as an American dance performer. The assimilation of techniques and expression continued in Tetley's other new works including *Ricercare* (1967), *Freefall* (1967), *Ziggurat* (1967), *Embrace Tiger and Return to Mountain* (1968) and *Rag Dances* (1971), highly influencing dancer-choreographers Norman Morrice, John Chesworth and Christopher Bruce. Tetley's choreography seemed to synthesize two genres to create something innovative and expressive.

For British dancers, this introduction to a synthesis of styles was not easy: Tetley 'made the spines work', wanted the dancers to take 'physical or mental risks', and demanded 'difficult floor work' which for some seemed like 'an abuse' of their classical training (Whitley, 2000). Yet Tetley's mix of dance language extended both content and expression in choreography, and had a liberating effect on narrative structure. Though *Pierrot Lunaire* is dramatically and structurally straightforward, his next work, *Freefall*, began without scenario or preconceived direction, to achieve a freefall of associations and relationships between people. Thus Tetley made an abstract work of no specific situation or narrative for two men and three women, involving solos, duets and double duets, created with its own dance language, and without imposing an established internal or external structure. Nevertheless audience and critics were touched by the expression of the work.

Since Tetley's training in America comprised improvisation and composition as well as technique, he tended to work through improvisation himself and then 'turn it over to the dancers ... to see what they will do with it' (Clarke and Crisp, 1974: 59). This approach places part responsibility on each dancer, offering a different experience from the more traditional interpretative expectations that they were used to. In introducing aspects of the American dance culture to Britain, Tetley introduced different conventions of dance lighting, design, costume and music. He brought an informed knowledge and acceptance of contemporary arts and their interdisciplinary usage which became the norm in the works of the Ballet Rambert, post-1966. Elements such as the use of film and mixed media, contemporary music and the influence of sculptors and painters on sets and designs, spawned a cross-fertilization of ideas and a focus on experimentation.

Also by the 1960s, changes had occurred in the roles of men in dance in the UK. Athleticism and strength countered the accepted dynamic range and gender-specific roles and vocabulary of the classical tradition; both men and women contributed to the new dance languages and partner work was also challenged. Perhaps the presence and charisma of Rudolf Nureyev as regular guest artist at the Royal Ballet contributed to this shift, with his dazzling virtuosity and controlled expressiveness.

In 1974 John Chesworth replaced Morrice as Director of the Ballet Rambert, with Christopher Bruce as Associate Director. The creation of new work with contemporary, social and personal themes continued, with eclectic use of modern dance languages. The ideas, themes and choreographic methods within the Rambert Company added to the importance of its role in the ensuing development of contemporary dance in Britain.

Meanwhile, across London, the philanthropist Robin Howard (who had so enjoyed Martha Graham's performances in Europe) set up the Contemporary Ballet Trust and founded the London School of Contemporary Dance (LSCD). With the appointment of Robert Cohan from the Graham Company as Artistic Director of the Trust, the School and the Company, yet again one individual initiated the growth of a new style of dance by implanting ideas from another country:

> Within only a short time a centre for artistic experiment had been established. Far more than a school for training dancers and dance teachers in Graham-based work, the LSCD spawned its own creative counter-movement and became the centre for choreographic experiment in Britain.
>
> (Jordan, 1992: 13)

Howard believed in cultivating rebellion and counter-movements within the institution and initially the LSCD attracted a mixed group of students, some interested in fine art, alternative theatre or performance art. Experimental work was encouraged, fired by the momentum of a heightened political consciousness, liberation and the development of the women's movement (Adair, 1992: 183). The results of this experimentation radically influenced the development of theatre dance in Europe.

As sole Artistic Director, Cohan provided the majority of works. His role was multifaceted: he taught, performed, choreographed and directed, with a 'non-aggressive authority' and a 'ready willingness to give other people opportunities' (Drummond, 1996: 11). At the time he saw his role as one of establishing a good technical base for the company, and Cohan's teaching of technique was generally praised, stimulated by his own technical capability and performance experience.

Graham-based technique and composition training methods devised by Louis Horst formed the basis of the course, supported by Jane Dudley and Nina Fonaroff (Jordan, 1992: 15). Cohan (1967: 19) chose not to fuse ballet with contemporary dance, as Tetley had done. Initially, works from choreographers who had worked with Graham – Cohan himself, Lapzeson, Louther and Powell – dominated London Contemporary Dance Theatre (LCDT) programmes. Cohan's works created between 1969 and 1977 included *Cell* (1969), *Stages* (1971, a full-length multimedia work), *Mass* (1973), *Waterless Method of Swimming Instruction* (1974), *Class* (1975), *Stabat Mater* (1975), *Nympheas* (1976), *Khamsin* (1976) and *Forest* (1977). The stated aim was to build 'a distinctively British repertory and thus give the company its own character' (Percival, 1980: 72), but in the early days, between 1969 and 1977, a predominantly American repertoire was occasionally enlivened with pieces by Richard Alston, Siobhan Davies and Micha Bergese.

The modernist aesthetic and symbolism demonstrated in many of them was perceived by the critics as reflecting an over-reliance on Graham's methods in terms of themes, language and form (Williams, 1969: 24). Evidently in his teaching of composition and performance, Cohan worked from similar principles to those he had encountered through Graham and Horst (Madden, 1996: 82). But by recognizing that the craft of choreography needed to be taught in the UK, and by ensuring that some basic rules of composition were passed on to members of his company, he empowered many dancers of the company, some of whom became choreographers in their own right, such as Robert North, Siobhan Davies and Richard Alston.

Cohan's own choreography was often labelled conventional, however, and he was praised more for his flair for production and scenographic theatrical effect, particularly in *Cell, Stages* and *Waterless Method of Swimming Instruction* (Percival, 1980: 72). Christopher Bannerman, who joined the company in 1975, confirms that Cohan still replicated codified movement from the Graham technique, at times equating dance with symbolic and representational gesture, and suggests that 'Bob's inextricable link between movement and emotion was both a positive and negative thing' (Bannerman, 2000). It was as if he saw his primary role as transmitting the Graham legacy to the UK, rather than allowing himself the freedom to develop his own artistry. Fergus Early described the LCDT company as

> never a radical force, being concerned to create a dance style, an audience and indeed a respectability to rival those of the ballet. In this it succeeded, and is both respectable and popular and in its way a pillar of the dance establishment.
>
> (Early, 1987: 11)

As a celebration of the virtuosity reached by the company after six years, *Class* (1975) presented in choreographic form all the movements and patterns that come from the daily technique class. Drummond suggests that for Cohan, choreography was rarely a question of narrative, but rather of a psychological perception, of the interaction of situation and personality (Drummond, 1996: 10–12). Certainly Bannerman recalled the 'multiplicity of meanings and feelings in his pieces', Cohan's hunches and his use of imagery to guide his negotiation with the dancers.

Stabat Mater (1975) was seen as a turning point in that the choreography transcended its form and content. The work was inspired by the first line of a poem by Jacopone da Todi: 'The Mother, sorrowing, stood weeping near the cross while her Son was hanging', and Cohan was inspired by the concept of actively standing still and sorrowing. His intent was for all the dancers to represent parts of Mary's experience rather than being attendants to her. Bannerman, who watched many rehearsals during the 10 days that it took to complete the work, commented that the theme and the classical music inspired the creation of 'a different language', one which seemed to be moving towards 'a fusion of style', and that the 'structural idea made the work clear and strong' (Bannerman, 2000). Cohan utilized the structure of the music, and the dance is carefully crafted around each section (Hodgens, 1975). For Drummond, '*Stabat Mater* had the authentic feeling of a deeply considered dance classic' (1996: 11).

Cohan's company LCDT closed in 1994 but his legacy remains. He contributed to the idea of choreography as a profession, taught dance composition and generously supported many young choreographers, including those who brought contrasting works to the LCDT repertoire, to ensure the development of contemporary dance in Britain.

POST-MODERN DANCE IN THE USA

Since the late 1960s, American post-modern dancer-choreographers have redefined and radicalized dance practice by challenging the orthodoxy of certain dominant ideologies – notions of excellence, elitism, the idealization of the body and hierarchical structures. Banes offers a definition of post-modernism in dance in *Terpsichore in Sneakers*:

> In dance, the confusion the term 'post-modern' creates is complicated by the fact that historical modern dance was never truly *modernist*. Often it has been precisely in the arena of post-modern dance that issues of modernism in the other arts have arisen: the acknowledgement of the medium's materials, the revealing of dance's essential qualities as an art form, the separation of formal elements, the abstraction of forms, and the elimination of external references as subjects. Thus in many respects it is post-modern dance that functions as *modernist* art. And yet, there are also aspects of post-modern dance that do fit with post-modernist notions (in the other arts) of pastiche, irony, playfulness, historical reference, the use of vernacular material, the continuity of cultures, an interest in process over product, breakdowns of boundaries between art forms and between art and life, and new relationships between artist and audience.
>
> (Banes, 1987: xv)

Banes identifies recognizable characteristics in post-modern dance in America from the 'breakaway' period of the early 1960s, to the transitional period of 1968–1973, the 'analytic' and 'metaphor and metaphysical' periods of the 1970s and the 'rebirth of content' in the 1980s. This development is well documented in her *Terpsichore in Sneakers: Post-Modern Dance* (1987), *Democracy's Body: Judson*

Dance Theater 1962–64 (1983) and *Writing Dancing in the Age of Post-modernism* (1994); Livet's *Contemporary Dance* (1978); Kaye's *Post-modernism and Performance* (1994); and Burt's *Judson Dance Theatre* (2006).

The 'breakaway' post-modern choreographers attempted to purge and ameliorate the vocabularies, symbolism and hierarchies of the modern dance and ballet: a 'spirit of permissiveness and playful rebellion prevailed' (Banes, 1987: xvii). They looked back at their heritage with irony (such as Rainer's screaming fit in a pile of white tulle in *Three Seascapes* (1962)), and used uninflected movements or untrained bodies. For example, Paxton's *Flat* (1964) challenged the use of space (art gallery, loft or parking lot instead of proscenium arch theatre), made the body itself the subject of the dance (nudity, violent Contact Improvisation), and used games, sports and contests as dance material. For these choreographers, a dance was a dance because of its context, not its content; that is, because it was framed as a dance.

Demystification was examined in two contrasting ways; either the body was dehumanized, as in Rauschenberg's *Pelican* (1963) or Child's *Carnation* (1964), or the body was venerated through an insistence on 'pure corporeality', as in Brown's *Trillium* (1962) or *Lightfall* (1963). The notion of 'letting go' in terms of technique or clothing, or the breaking of other accepted dance conventions such as the use of tension or control in the body, was apparent in the nudity of Brown and Paxton's *Word Words* (1963) or the explicit sexual imagery of Carolee Schneemann's *Meat Joy* (1964). Improvisation was often employed on stage, signalling a previously unknown freedom in choreography.

The years between 1968 and 1973 were a transitional period during which time more overtly political themes were engaged and works became explicitly didactic, such as Rainer's *War* (1970) and many of Paxton's pieces. The Grand Union, a collective for improvisation, gave a benefit performance for the Black Panthers, and in 1972 Paxton and others began Contact Improvisation, an alternative technique but also 'social network'. Eastern movement philosophies, dance-drama genres and the martial arts also began to influence post-modern dance. By 1973, a recognizable style had emerged as dominant, 'one that was reductive, factual, objective and down-to-earth', which Banes (1987) labels 'analytic post-modern dance'.

In 1975 Michael Kirby published an issue of *The Drama Review* which was devoted to this form of post-modern dance, a form that rejected musicality, meaning, characterization, mood and atmosphere. Following Cunningham's 1960–1970 phase, expressive effects or overt references were stripped away, and devices such as accumulation, reversal and repetition created conceptual challenges analogous with the values of minimalism in the visual arts. Audiences were confronted with the material of the dance, the movement, and the process of making pieces, as for example in Trisha Brown's *Accumulation Pieces* (from 1971 to 1978), Lucinda Child's *Calico Mingling* (1973) or the revelation of the conditions of performance demonstrated by Grand Union.

A contrasting set of characteristics in the 1970s sprang from an appreciation of non-Western aesthetic dance forms, which Banes categorized as 'metaphoric and metaphysical' post-modern dance. She refers here to dance that had a spiritual or religious function, like Halprin's 'rituals' or Hay's Circle dances, reminiscent of Laban's movement choirs of pre-Second World War Germany. Metaphoric post-modern dance also includes Kenneth King's use of dance as 'metaphors for technology, information and power systems' which reflect technological developments as they impinge on American society.

At the end of the 1970s there was a return to meaning and expression in post-modern dance in America through 'the rebirth of content', a departure from the asceticism of analytic post-modern dance towards some of the issues prevalent in modern dance. The works of dancer/choreographers such as Molissa Fenley and Karole Armitage required a strong technique together with strength and speed of a virtuoso nature; themes, music and costume reflected the social mores of the 1980s, and dance pieces often appropriated language and media systems. Narrative and autobiographical material stimulated or accompanied dances, but the basic difference which made content-based post-modern dance dissimilar from modern dance lay in the structuring of the material. Works tended to be specifically non-linear, juxtaposing image and expression, thus allowing individual responses from audiences rather than giving them collective theatrical experiences.

THE LIBERATING CHARACTERISTICS OF NEW DANCE IN BRITAIN

In *Out of Line: The Story of British New Dance*, Judith Mackrell begins by attempting a definition of New Dance, and concluding, 'no single ideology and no single approach to choreography has dominated the movement' (Mackrell, 1992: 1). She quotes Fergus Early's manifesto: 'New Dance is not: baggy trousers, rolling about, chinese shoes, contact improvisation, ballet to rock music, release work, image work, outside performances, post-modern dance, martial arts, self-indulgence, American, non-narrative.' Early concluded, 'the one and only essential concept to New Dance is Liberation' (Early, 1987: 10–12).

This notion of liberation is viewed in relation to the established conventions and perceived restraints of ballet and modern dance in the 1960s and 1970s. While it is simplistic to identify the movement with a single philosophy of liberation, certain characteristics can be distinguished, some of which relate to developments in American post-modern dance already mentioned. These include a shift towards individuality in movement choices, eclecticism of dance language, juxtaposition of structural devices, and a further move towards the interaction of dance with the culture, economics and politics of its day.

First, liberation was concerned with an interest in the body and dance language, and in the comparison between a technically trained body and an untrained one. Individuality might mean idiosyncratic movement, a personal movement style very different from a codified dance language. On the one hand, this led to pedestrian movement and enjoyment of the untrained body; or to a search for new ways of moving, from street and folk forms to 'borrowing' dances and movement from other cultures; to a fusion of two or more dance styles, or the freedom of improvisation, alone or in contact with a partner. In the 1970s, 'alternative attitudes' to the body included release work, Contact Improvisation, the Alexander Technique and various forms of martial art including tai chi, aikido and capoeira. Dancer/choreographers chose to demystify the body by using everyday gesture, task-based improvisation, and non-dancers in performance; their delight in the unenhanced body was principally a revolt against conventional training by those who had been through the system and therefore had something to reject.

Contact Improvisation certainly reverses the process of external image in classical or contemporary dance, based as it is in the physical laws of mass, gravity, momentum and inertia, and demanding sensitivity, support and accommodation between two people. Non-dancers can quickly become adept at it, and as a social model it offers equality. In the 1970s Contact Improvisation became a recognizable characteristic of many New Dance pieces, often used to link certain fixed points in the choreography. In partnerships like those of Julyen Hamilton and Kirstie Simson, notable skill, virtuosity and intuition were developed. For example, each performance of *Agatha and Jimmy* (1985) was different from the one preceding it. Simson described the risk of improvisation in performance: 'I have a feeling that we are dealing with performance and material in a very multi-dimensional way where you can't have control over it, you just have to let it be' (Burt, 1985: 10).

Second, liberation refers to the themes or issues chosen by dance practitioners: permissiveness, rebellion and ironic or surreal use of the dance heritage or a more factual approach to dance-making to challenge the expressionist or modernist norms. Challenges to the establishment embraced overt political themes, social issues or explicit sexual imagery, and subverted the highly stylized gestures of modern dance.

Themes and issues chosen by New Dance practitioners were wide-ranging and eclectic. Some deconstructed the classical heritage, like Fergus Early and Jacky Lansley: Lansley's *Swan Lake Act 2* (1976), Early's *Naples* (1978), Lansley and Rose English's *Juliet and Juliet a Duet, Romeo and Romeo a Duel* (1979) and *I, Giselle* (1980), co-directed by Lansley and Early. A number of works engaged with feminist strategies, the conditioned persona and image of the female dancer, the roles of women, or menstruation and pregnancy. For example, Lansley's *Dance Object* (1977), *Bleeding Fairies* (1977), a collaboration between Emilyn Claid, Lansley and Mary Prestidge; and Claid's *Making a Baby* (1979), performed when she was seven months pregnant. There were also a number of works which drew on individuals' autobiographical details, such as Claid's *Going Back* (1976), *Family Background* (1977) by Sarah Green, and

Maedee Duprès's *Choice and Presence* (1977), which explored imagery from her childhood in Switzerland.

Third, in terms of form and structure, liberation meant that chance ideas were used to generate or organize dance content, or that the microstructure of the dance was created through organic, collage or layering techniques, or that formal filmic devices were used, such as accumulation, reversal or repetition. Traditional ideas about dance structure were sometimes superseded by the juxtaposition of unrelated, discrete sections of separate materials that created a deliberate jarring effect, or distanced movement from a recognizable personal style.

Inherent in these ideas about liberation was an intrinsic question of meaning, and shifts in audience response. New Dance demanded response on both an empathetic *and* an intellectual level; within a choreographic work, many possibilities of meaning exist that may or may not be intentional. In contrast with the 'unified' product offered by establishment ballet and modern dance companies, New Dance works tended to be constructed through organic or collage structures, non-linear narratives, or by deliberate juxtapositioning of discrete sections of separate material. *Manley Struggles* (1978), a piece by Fergus Early and Julian Hough, is an example where 'the whole structure was a kind of linear collage, a constant dialectic. Internal and external comment was stimulated through theatrical means (e.g. playing on the rehearsed/spontaneous relationship of the actors/people)' (Hayes, 1978: 6).

Like the post-moderns, New Dance practitioners tended to be questioning, consciousness-raising and unorthodox, critical of the mainstream and reflective of each other. Discussion and debate became an educative force, manifested in the development of more articulate dancers who also choreographed, in new forms of critical writing in the journal *New Dance*, and in sharing and critiquing each other's choreographic work in progress. Thus organizations like X6 challenged the perceived mindlessness of some forms of highly technical dance training, and initiated the link between dance-making and research, possibly one of British New Dance's most important characteristics.

Collaborative pieces were common, often exploring political issues of sexism, elitism or feminism, or the ideological situation of arts practice. *Mounting* (1977), a collaborative piece by Rose

English, Jacky Lansley and Sally Potter, dealt with arts practice and its relation to women artists. Claire Hayes consistently made pieces about feminine issues, as in *Sphinx* (1980); in the same programme Anna Furse investigated such issues as oppression and patriarchal systems in *Under* (1980). Because the social relationships of groupings and collaborations were immensely flexible and determined by availability of personnel, most New Dance works were not more than 60–70 minutes in length; one-night performances toured for a few months only and were then discarded.

The growth of small groups and pick-up companies in the 1980s meant that a gradually increasing pool of experienced dancers was able to contribute to the creation and development of new pieces. The opportunity of working with the same choreographer over a period of time, in informal settings, provided contexts in which the specific choreographic concerns and stylistic qualities of a choreographer could be explored more deeply.

Mackrell identified the very close alignment of these pieces to the post-modern tradition in dance 'in which fragmentation, subversion, casualness and anti-expression are now such key terms' (Mackrell, 1984: 30). Mary Fulkerson's piece *Fine Romance* (1983), shown in the 1983 Dance Umbrella, incorporated elements of narrative that were persistently fragmented and subverted. Mackrell wrote that 'the piece suggested a surreal parody of a conventional musical' (1984: 30).

Peter Hall suggested that fragmentation was the most fertile possible environment for the arts, and recognized the debt that the establishment owed fringe theatre (Appleyard, 1984: 85). This same phenomenon can be identified in the field of dance in terms of the non-linear structuring devices that were chosen by practitioners from the New Dance genre, and that remain a feature of independent dance-making. It is evident that ideas that germinated in the avant-garde of both London and New York have subsequently been transmitted from group to group, much as in Chinese whispers, borrowed, personalized and passed on, while new knowledge is introduced from other countries, ethnic groups, social or martial forms. Eventually choreographers and dancers within the more established companies have subsumed some of these ideas, and much of what was initiated in the 1970s and 1980s has essentially become part of the fabric of the domain of choreographic process today.

PINA BAUSCH AND THE GERMAN SCENE

The twentieth century witnessed two unique dance forms which emerged in Germany. In the 1930s *Ausdruckstanz* viewed dance as a philosophical and spiritual assertion, while *Tanztheater*, which emerged in West Germany in the 1970s 'featured body and movement in the discourse of the psyche and society, everyday behaviour and its norm' (Grau and Jordan, 2000: 55–56). The new choreographers emphasized corporal expression and visual poetry at the expense of formal concerns and displays of virtuosity. Former students of Mary Wigman, such as Susanne Linke and Gerhard Bohner, and alumni of the Folkwang School in Essen like Reinhild Hoffmann and Pina Bausch became the new pioneers. There was a return to solo dance and an interest in improvisation as a tool of creative construction (Manning and Benson, 2001: 218). Thus the creative works of Rudolf Laban, Mary Wigman and Kurt Jooss are not just records of 'ceaseless probing, enquiry and experiment', but an important German dance heritage which influenced another generation of choreographers some 55 years later (Coton, 1975: 135).

In 1962, Pina Bausch joined Kurt Jooss's new Folkwang Ballett Company as a soloist and assisted Jooss on many choreographies, succeeding him as Artistic Director in 1969. In 1972, she became Artistic Director of the then Wuppertal Opera Ballet, later renamed the Tanztheater Wuppertal Pina Bausch.

Our current preoccupation with Bausch's work is perhaps coloured by an extraordinary oeuvre of over 30 full-length productions. With Tanztheater Wuppertal, she explored dance as a vehicle for socio-political meaning, approaching choreography with and through the personal experiences of her dancers. Like Brecht, Bausch wanted her spectators to think about what they saw and heard and to draw their own conclusions.

Through gestures, words and the use of repetition for deliberate effect, she applied all theatrical and dramaturgic means to decipher the male/female relationship or interaction, a theme found throughout her work. In her version of *The Rite of Spring* (1975) the choreography was highly physical and erotic; the entire stage was covered with peat so that one could not only see and hear but also smell the earthiness which characterized this production. In other works like *Bluebeard* (1977) or *Café Muller* (1978), the stage was covered with leaves, or with chairs, while male and female dancers incessantly reached out for each other, but their attempts at embracing and caressing made it painfully clear that there was no real communication. Bausch tended to use music collages, pre-recorded clips of music from old popular songs, folk songs, arias or classical music; costumes often evoked social reality of a period gone by – suits, high heels and evening gowns. Structurally, her works seem to have a theme which binds the short scenes together, but they could also be put together in any order so that they become more fragmented, more montage-like, more provocative.

Lloyd Newson said of Bausch, whose piece *1980 – Ein Stück von Pina Bausch* he first saw in London in 1982:

> Bausch understood that dance and linear narrative weren't always the best vehicles for discussing the human condition. Even if you were a disciple of her work from the outset, like I was, her work could delight you but just as easily frustrate and annoy you. That was her magnificence. Bausch made you feel. She had the courage to relentlessly pursue, on stage, her own fascinations and obsessions about time and human relations no matter how minuscule or epic those ideas might be; and that was her genius. It is rare to find dance- or theatre-makers with such vision and courage. Her work truly allowed people to see the world from another perspective that, had she not been around, we would never have known. Her legacy is monumental.
>
> (Newson, 2009)

The Tanztheater legacy has been taken up by many choreographers for whom Bausch was an inspiration: Lloyd Newson himself, with his company DV8; the Belgians Wim Wanderkeybus, Jan Fabre and Alain Platel (Ballets C de la B); Susanne Linke and Gerhard Bohner, Jasmin Vardimon and many others.

NEXT?

History advances every day. In 1999, Martha Bremser published *Fifty Contemporary Choreographers*, an authoritative guide to the lives and works of the prominent choreographers of that era. A reprint in 2011, co-edited with Lorna Sanders, has replaced several of those with other choreographers. But, out of necessity, both these editions are selective, choosing to document the biographies and works of artists about whom articles have already been written, and critical writing published. Dance-related courses are now so well established in so many universities and colleges around the world that there are many histories. Colleagues in Malaysia and Taiwan, Hawaii and New Zealand, are documenting the dance events important to their society, their culture and their future. As such these will be *their* histories, selected to privilege one period over another, and thus both personal and partial.

Out of the hundreds of interesting dance-makers in this first decade of the twenty-first century, across the globe, my personal choices include those who have established their own styles, and whose histories I look forward to following further:

> William Forsythe, American, based in Frankfurt am Main, Germany
> Wayne McGregor, Random Dance and Royal Ballet, London
> Akram Khan, London and Singapore
> Belgian-based American choreographer Meg Stuart
> French choreographer Jérôme Bel
> Taiwan-based choreographer Lin Hwai-min of Cloud Gate Dance Theatre

As Dance Studies students, you will no doubt be introduced to dance history and study some of the resources mentioned here. But you will also investigate many choreographic developments of your own era and location, and no doubt these will be personal and partial, just like mine.

FURTHER READING/RESEARCH

Look up all the practitioners and genres/styles mentioned on www. youtube.com

Bremser, Martha and Lorna Sanders (2011) *Fifty Contemporary Choreographers* second edition London and New York: Routledge

Climenhaga, Royd (2009) *Pina Bausch* London and New York: Routledge

Manning, Susan (1993) *Ecstasy and the Demon: Feminism and Nationalism in the Dances of Mary Wigman* Berkeley, Calif.: University of California Press

Newhall, Mary Anne Santos (2009) *Mary Wigman* London and New York: Routledge

Partsch-Bergsohn, Isa and Harold Bergsohn (2002). *The Makers of Modern Dance in Germany: Rudolf Laban, Mary Wigman, Kurt Jooss* Princeton, NJ: Princeton Book Company

4

PERFORMING DANCES

Contained within the notion that all dance is made (created, choreographed) is the idea that each particular dance requires a series of physical and expressive capacities before it can be performed. Both the physical and the expressive competencies alike are directly related to the work's context and function. This area of activity we call performance, and in Dance Studies at the undergraduate level it usually includes the act of showing, demonstrating or performing in front of an audience of peers or others relevant to the student's class work. This might mean the performance of a technical assignment in class, the performance of a solo in a studio theatre or a large ensemble production on stage or on tour. Different forms of preparation are pertinent to each of these modes, and parts of your programme of study will be dedicated to appropriate methods. We learn to perform only to serve the intentions of the makers and as makers ourselves, to be free to realize our own intentions. *The acquisition of performance skills is not an end in itself.*

In addition to the technical skills that dancers learn in classes, the dancer in performance needs to develop other important attributes that contribute to becoming an all-round performer. Understandings about style, interpretation, musicality, expression, focus and projection can all be introduced through dance technique and choreography sessions, but it is only through experiencing the choreographic process and preparing for performance that this capacity can be fully developed. Dancers have personal qualities and physical differences that can become important aspects of the choreographer's inspiration. Indeed, these differences are often identified at the audition stage. In the preparation for performance, the relationship between dancers and choreographer in the studio is two-way, a specific kind of dialogue.

The dancer needs to understand the intention and style of the choreographer, the nuances of the dance material, and his or her own abilities in the embodiment, transformation and communication of the completed dance. Some of this is dependent on the ways in which the choreographer shares information in the rehearsal room.

Other elements too become important in performance; examples include the interrelationships on stage and the ways in which the dancers connect as an ensemble, the particular location of the performance and the inherent qualities of the space, and the relationship of sound and scenography with the dance. All these elements have an effect upon the audience as they observe and absorb the interacting elements of a dance performance. But first, dancers have to be selected.

AUDITION

How do choreographers choose their dancers? Imagine attending an audition of 300 dancers or more – and wondering what the choreographer might be looking for. Of course, the ability to pick up the steps and perform them as demonstrated is assumed; but there are many other factors that affect the choice. For example, does a dancer have the physical attributes that will suit the personal signature style of the choreographer or the character of the role? Does the dancer have long legs, or a strong torso, an articulate spine or expressive arms, if these attributes are important? Does the dancer's unique persona come across in the audition, or does she have 'stage presence' or charisma? Could the dancer's physical attributes convey the vulnerability or sensuality of a particular character? And essentially, does the dancer have the required dynamic range, musicality and expressive potential, if those are what is required?

Companies have different needs when holding auditions. Stanton Welch, Artistic Director of Houston Ballet, advises that generally dancers need to be dressed appropriately, they need to learn the exercises with detail and show that they have a level of artistry. The company wants to see a broad range of your best qualities as an artist. 'What makes you stand out (at audition) is your work ethic and your artistry. You need to be a smart and intelligent dancer, as well as being someone who can completely transform into any role' (www.houstonballet.org).

Each choreographer perceives new dancers in relation to his or her own choreography and context: the company, other dancers, height and build, style and quality, etc. Is a certain physique or 'look' important? Is a feminine, masculine or androgynous body favoured? Do the male dancers need to be able to lift the females? These questions will no doubt affect the decision-making process. No doubt there are also some not-so-certain, more serendipitous elements to the choices made – perhaps a dancer with a particular intensity, vulnerability, confident presence or recognizable persona is needed.

The choreographer Wayne McGregor of Random Dance is quite clear that a choreographic process is an ideal example of 'distributed cognition' or shared understandings; he and his company are involved with a project at the University of California, San Diego, investigating how ideas are distributed and disseminated within a team:

> We looked at some seminal questions: during a [choreographic] process, which parts of an idea are retained by the group (or individual) and which parts are dropped? What mental models do we each develop when we improvise together? What forms of communication do we use to share, transform and vary the ideas and how is gesture, verbal language and sound utilised to embody the concepts?
>
> (Dietz, 2010)

McGregor and his dancers found that this research led to new frameworks and new points of departure in the rehearsal room: for example, sharing a richer understanding of the distinctions between visual, aural and kinaesthetic images and how they can be used to create dance. It is evident that, in addition to choosing dancers with a particular body shape and technical articulation, McGregor chooses dancers able to bring this independence of thought to the process.

Other questions in the audition, then, relate to methods of making, composing or reconstructing dances, and the style of the choreographer's artistic leadership. Some choreographers work closely with their dancers on the setting of tasks, improvisation, or problem-solving strategies, while others create movement material on their own bodies and are particularly interested in how quickly dance material can be picked up, absorbed and memorized. The job in hand is distinctly different if the choreography already exists in the repertoire of the company and a new dancer is being asked to step into a role; in this situation, the ability to learn dance material very fast, and retain it exactly, is a priority.

Let us consider the contribution that dancers can make in the creation of a new work by taking the example of William Forsythe, former Director of Ballett Frankfurt (1984–2004) and now director of the Forsythe Company (2005–present). His company structure has shifted away from more traditional choreographing towards creative collaboration in the company, allowing the dancers to make personal decisions and work independently. Ballett Frankfurt's repertoire increasingly involved choreographic input from other members of the company, either through intricate improvisation or scores and tasks, counterpoint and juxtaposition (Midgette, 2000: 16–17). Dana Caspersen, a colleague in the company, describes the dancer's role thus:

> Bill speaks of the Frankfurt Ballet as a choreographic ensemble. In many new productions the dancers are involved in several sides of the creative process, so he looks for artists and colleagues, people who are interested in his work, but who also have their own art hearts and minds and don't wait for orders. He looks for people with what I would term dance intelligence: curiosity, fearlessness, and the desire continuously to re-approach dancing.
>
> (2000: 25–26)

By engaging them in tasks to create their own movement material, and by relying on their spontaneity and creativity in improvisations and variations, he emancipates his dancers' status at the level of generating movement content. His own role may change with each production, but 'he can always be seen as a catalyst and editor'. He may initiate the improvisations, set conditions, or select movement created by dancers; he might organize and edit different layers of material, or design the overall structure of the choreography. As a dancer with this company, then, the competences required by dancers are quite distinctly beyond technical expertise.

Before attending an audition of any kind – to enter a university or college programme or a dance company – it is obviously important to prepare. Be pragmatic about examining your own needs and dreams, but also make an honest assessment of your capabilities. Are you good at picking up new material, remembering long sequences, responding to tasks? Do you enjoy experimenting, improvising for hours, expressing yourself freely, engaging in discussion? Research the course or company, find out what might be required of you and prepare some questions to ask. Be alert and learn as much as you can while you are there. Auditions are a two-way process!

In many Dance Studies programmes, final year students are often assessed on their ability to make choreography and so the audition procedure is one that you may choose to exploit to find dancers. Be clear about your intentions and your own preferred methods of working, work out what you are going to teach or how you want to facilitate improvisation, and identify what kinds of dancer you are looking for, but always be open to new possibilities.

LEARNING TO DANCE FROM THE INSIDE

Dance communicates best when it has the ability to evoke an aesthetic or an emotional response. Dances can be well performed and technically skilful, they can have extraordinary costumes, complex patterns of movement and sophisticated lighting design, but if there is no inner substance then we may as well be watching acrobatics. As Alma Hawkins (1991: 2) asks, what is it about a piece of choreography that causes the audience to be drawn into the experience, to respond imaginatively, and to feel aesthetic satisfaction? How do professionals do it – what strategies do they develop?

There is no short answer to this question, but many suggestions about how to proceed. Teachers and lecturers need to create a better learning environment for technique, choreography and performance training, where there can be a balance of didactic and discovery learning: where individuals can be helped and guided to make dance and perform roles that reflect their own unique experience. The preparation for this can take place in the rehearsal studio, but it can also take place through other enriching experiences like reading and researching, going to performances and exhibitions of other art forms, developing the art of conversation, travelling, and becoming more informed about politics, ecology, science and art. All students can be encouraged to be curious and to question.

Alma Hawkins introduces some important concepts for making and performing in her book *Moving from Within: A New Method for Dance Making* (1991), focusing on experiencing, expressing, feeling, transforming and evaluating. She strongly suggests that young dancers and dance-makers require both structure and freedom;

> *structure* in the sense of a framework that encourages the discovery of concepts and truths related to the artistic process; *freedom* in the sense of the opportunity to explore movement ideas and allow the imaginative transformation of experiences (inner vision) to take shape in an externalised form. The challenge is to provide a structure and learning environment that facilitates growth and at the same time protects the individual's freedom to take a hand in his or her own creative development and pursue personal goals with self-confidence.
>
> (Hawkins, 1991: 3)

This is possible in the integrated world of the university or college, where students develop some autonomy and can take responsibility for aspects of their education. But this approach to learning is perhaps more common in contemporary/modern dance education than in ballet. Deborah Bull accepts that ballet has an endemic problem, as the very nature of ballet training can tend to exclude creativity. Because ballet is such an exact art form, dancers are trained to understand a 'right' and 'wrong' way of doing things.

> If they are writing off the 'wrong' way, they are writing off their own creativity. Essentially you are trying to reproduce exactly the positions and dynamics of the ways of moving that people have produced before. It is the antithesis of creativity.

There is a problem, but the problem I am particularly interested in is the problem within the training.
(www.ballet.co.uk/magazines/yr_02/.../interview_deborah_
bull.htm)

In the last 10 years, however, much has changed. The curricula of most of the vocational schools and colleges for dance have begun to adapt to the changing needs of the profession. Increasingly choreographers seek a range of opportunities that allow them to move between genres such as contemporary dance, opera, community dance, musicals and ballet, where they can hone and apply their skills, develop their vocabularies and adapt their respective processes. Dancers need to understand and to be able to supplement new work; skills of improvisation and knowledge of compositional processes can aid their comprehension of, and contribution to the choreographic process. Boundaries are blurring, and contemporary dance-makers now incorporate an extraordinarily eclectic range of styles, forms and techniques. Dancers need to be ready for this challenge.

We experience our world through constant interchange of sensory data which come from seeing, hearing, touching, smelling, tasting; and through movement, weight, speed and space; and through our emotions. We learn through our social interactions, our culture, our heritage, and through the people with whom we interact. And I think that these experiences help to inform the development of the choreographer, the dancer, the performer. Essentially, preparation for performance is a creative act as much as a technical one. The dancer draws on his or her memories, thoughts, sensations and imagination to formulate modes of expression that feel appropriate to the role or the character. Ideas are tried out in the privacy of the studio, shared with fellow dancers, developed, retried. I feel sure that the ability to be both curious and creative is one of the layering processes that contribute towards a dancer becoming an artist.

THE DANCER'S CONTRIBUTION TO EXISTING CHOREOGRAPHY

Most major ballet and modern dance companies own choreographic works which remain in the repertoire for a number of years. Young dancers take on the roles of those who retire or move on to other companies, sometimes being coached by older, experienced dancers. But as Leanne Benjamin says, 'it is not easy stepping into other people's roles – you need to bring your own thoughts and interpretation to it'. Tamara Rojo is also adamant that it is 'essential to make a role your own' and that one of the many ways of doing it is to develop the technique by adding more pirouettes or extensions, or developing the dramatic intensity. Ed Watson makes clear that a role does not remain static but builds from season to season: 'the roles get better as you build on your knowledge ... ideas come to you during the performance', and these refinements become part of the layering process. Individuality is an important aspect: Lauren Cuthbertson warns that dancers should not try to copy or emulate others, but find something individual to bring to a role (www.roh.org.uk).

The dancer in performance needs to be able to communicate the overall intention of the dance, but ideally to bring something unique, perhaps charismatic, to the role. So, apart from being able to learn the steps and perform them adequately, what other attributes do dancers bring to the rehearsal room? How does a dancer learn to interpret and communicate the dance? How can dancers ensure that what they dance reaches out from the body and 'touches' the audience's sensibilities or feelings? What powers of projection, focus and awareness does s/he need?

The French ballerina Sylvie Guillem's approach to preparation for a role can be seen in a specially made TV programme about her career. In 1993, the *South Bank Show*, which was a regular culture programme on ITV for many years, hosted by Melvyn Bragg, produced a one-hour programme on Guillem. She is an exceptionally gifted performer, thoughtful, intelligent and instinctual, who left the Paris Opéra Ballet in 1989 for a guest contract with London's Royal Ballet so that she could have the freedom to accept invitations to dance with other international companies. The programme provides many insights into the challenges of her career: the sense of stifling ownership of the Paris Opéra in the 1980s, her own desire for independence, the controlling attitude of some choreographers and critics who prefer to maintain tradition and respect for the set choreography rather than to allow a creative performer to alter any steps ... This story is one of a charismatic and independent dancer with an exceptional technique, constantly looking for new challenges, who evidently did not choose to approach the major classical ballet roles in the same way that other dancers did.

As John Percival suggests (*South Bank Show*, 1993), nobody wants to hear every actor come on and intone the words the same way, and nobody wants a dancer to dance the steps the same way. 'They want to see the steps properly done, but they want to see them phrased and inflected in a way that is unique, something surprising and of the moment.' But it is obvious that many people felt that Guillem had gone too far in altering the choreography for her own purposes, and adding very high extensions to roles that were not conceived that way. Her tendency to do what her instinct told her sometimes conflicted with the requirements of the choreographer.

A good example of a role that has been performed with a number of interpretations is the dramatic narrative work *Manon* (1974) by Kenneth MacMillan, an epic ballet of love, luxury and passion. Set in decadent eighteenth-century Paris, the young, beautiful and naïve Manon is torn between two lives; privilege and opulence with the wealthy Guillot Morfontaine or innocent love with the penniless student Des Grieux. In terms of the performance of the central character, Manon herself has altered as different dancers have taken on the role:

> Antoinette Sibley saw her as a girl 'who allowed it all to happen to her ... I don't think she's a schemer – she only makes decisions when she has to'. Lynn Seymour made her more ruthless: she and her brother are 'cut from the same cloth, both bandits, using all they have to achieve what they want ... she broke the rules and the punishment crushed her'. Natalia Makarova understood her as an instinctive creature who lives for the moment, 'extracting from it all the excitement she can. At the same time she fully knows that the day will come when she must pay the price ... for the pleasure of living fully'. Sylvie Guillem's guileful *Manon* used her sexual allure to survive in a male-dominated world. Des Grieux's misfortune was to have strayed into her path just as she was discovering her power. Where other *Manon*s die as desperate victims, limp as rags, Guillem fought on, defying death itself.
>
> (www.kennethmacmillan.com)

COACHING

Through the mechanism of 'coaching' that is employed in most of the major dance companies, we can understand how a distinctive choreographic style can be maintained and transmitted. Experienced dancers develop these roles, and pass on their skill and knowledge of style, characterization, technical demands, personal mastery and expertise. Monica Mason, Director of the Royal Ballet, can be viewed coaching the soloist Kristen McNally in the role of Carabosse, the wicked fairy godmother in *The Sleeping Beauty*. Focusing on expressing character, and forwarding the narrative through gesture and dynamic, Mason solicits a vindictive energy, fake politeness towards the King and Queen, and a delightful feeling of triumph as Carabosse reveals her spell. Mason even dances a short section, indicating her deep knowledge of, and familiarity with, the role (www.roh.org.uk).

A further example comes from the National Ballet of Canada where John Cranko's ballet *Onegin* was restaged for the 2011 season. This work was created by Cranko for the Stuttgart Ballet in 1965 from an adaptation of the verse novel *Eugene Onegin* by Alexander Pushkin, set to music by Tchaikovsky and orchestrated by Kurt-Heinz Stolze. It is a dramatic, tragic work, full of emotional intensity, layering themes of passion, honour and regret. Reid Anderson, currently the Artistic Director of the Stuttgart Ballet, danced the role of Onegin there in the 1960s, and has staged it in Canada before. Recently he has been coaching two principals from the National Ballet of Canada – Ji Jelinek and Xiao Nan Yu – in the roles of Onegin and Tatiana (www.national.ballet.ca). In four short video clips, the public can find out about the new designs and costumes and see the company in rehearsal.

Another valuable example of coaching (available online) is on the Kenneth MacMillan website, where Lynn Seymour coaches Tamara Rojo of the Royal Ballet in the role of Juliet for the ballet *Romeo and Juliet* (1965). Seymour was MacMillan's muse for the making of this role, and we learn much about the specific style required and the technical adjustments that had to be made by the ballerina in order to project the feeling of being off balance and slightly out of control. Seymour finds appropriate imagery to aid the desired quality and dynamic, and what is quite evident here from the dialogue between Seymour and Rojo is that coaching is a two-way process designed to transmit the original intentions of the choreographer while finding the best way for a ballerina to interpret the role (www.kennethmacmillan.com).

An issue which becomes very apparent when discussing coaching is the discrimination which occurs between the large, publicly funded companies and the smaller project-funded ensembles. Whereas the companies have infrastructure and resources to maintain their repertoires and support new soloists to gain access to these roles – such as double or treble casting, understudying, rehearsal directors, notators/choreologists, coaching opportunities – the small annually funded dance groups have no such support. If dancers are ill or injured, and there is no understudy, it is likely that the choreography will be changed at the last minute to accommodate the problem. Dancers have phenomenal movement memories and they often have improvisatory and interpretative skills that allow them to cope with such spontaneous reactions. Contemporary dancers tend to be creative in different ways to their ballet counterparts; they may well have more experience of different forms of improvisation which may be used to generate new dance content in the creative, choreographic context. Yet these 'pick-up' dancers give so much of themselves in terms of talent and capability to companies that cannot afford to employ them full time, where there is little hope of maintaining a role, or having the time to fully embody a character.

For dance students, the opportunities presented by being coached by an expert are valuable, as is demonstrated by Tresa Randall from the Ohio University School of Dance:

> The Ohio University School of Dance has been thrilled to participate in the Nikolais Centennial by performing Noumenon. The students learned so much from Tito during his short residency here, when he coached them in the extreme clarity of line, control of energy, and sensitivity to time required by the work. We are so pleased to have the Nikolais/Louis archives housed here, and performing Noumenon has enabled our students to deepen their understanding of Nikolais' work and theories even further.
>
> (www.nikolaislouis.org)

LIVING THE EXPERIENCE

The embodiment of movement by performers is a complex process:

> It is more than getting movement into the dancers' bodies, more than their physical muscle, bone and skin. Embodiment of movement involves the whole person, a person conscious of being a living body, living that experience, giving intention to the movement material.
>
> (Preston-Dunlop and Sanchez-Colberg, 2002: 7)

Embodying a role requires a dancer to adapt his habitual motor patterns in order to assimilate the requirements of the choreographer.

In 1992, Birmingham Royal Ballet engaged Anna Markard, the daughter of Kurt Jooss, to reconstruct Jooss's *The Green Table* (1932) on the company. Joseph Cipolla was cast as the figure of Death. Over six weeks, 'the sensate, intellectual, emotional embodiment took place: a gradual painstaking process in which minute detail of Jooss' style needed to become part of the lived experience of Cipolla' (2002: 9). Cipolla had to relinquish his normal classical movement, and learn to use weight and rhythm in the manner of the choreography of this character of Death, created in 1930s Germany. Note here two relevant issues: first, that if someone does not protect the particular stylistic and physical requirements of the choreography, and take great care in the reconstruction of a work, then the particular quality of the original will not be maintained. Here, Anna Markard is the guardian of her father's work. Second, the craft and artistry of Joseph Cipolla is challenged by a style of dance which is distinctly different from the style in which he was trained. We become aware of the depth of commitment required in order to fully embody a role which emanated from a different time and place. There is certainly no room to be concerned with ego in this situation: the artist consciously involves himself in exploration of a very different kind of performative context.

THE DANCER'S CONTRIBUTION TO NEW CHOREOGRAPHY

As we begin to realize, the relationship between the dancers and choreographer in the studio determines the future of the dance itself. The lines of communication between them, the nature and depth of the demonstration, the quality of the verbal articulation, the trust, the attitude, all these determine how the dancer will respond to the requirements of the choreographer. The dancer's intelligence and understanding are related to the choreographer's ability to articulate what is required, their creative interrelationship and the ability of both to problem-solve.

Valda Setterfield, who danced with Merce Cunningham, describes his choreographic method:

> My memory of it, particularly with my *Walkaround Time* (1968) solo and also *Changing Steps* (1975) is that Merce didn't show me *anything*. In fact, for my *Walkaround Time* solo, he sat in a chair the whole time and said: 'Can you do this? Can you try that? And maybe a little of this, and the other?' It was quite marvellous because I never saw it on anybody else's body – which, no matter how objective you can be, colours your sensibility about it.
>
> (Kostelanetz, 1992: 103)

Here, although there was no demonstration, Setterfield was very familiar with Cunningham's vocabulary through working on material in class, and having performed in another of his works. She obviously relished the opportunity to contribute at a personal level to the making of this solo.

Gus Solomons, who also danced with the Cunningham company, remembers learning dance phrases in class,

> but I have very little recollection of how we learned solo parts and other things. I guess Merce demonstrated them and then right away *extracted* from us individually what he wanted to see. In other words, he would give us an indication of the movement; 'This is a hip circle here' – and then he would watch us do it and say how it was wrong and how he wanted it to be done. For me the process was almost invisible.
>
> (Kostelanetz, 1992: 102)

Cunningham's general philosophy about making work usually starts with a question to solve. In conversation with Jacqueline Lesschaeve, he explains his perspective:

You deal with people and they are also your material. I never felt the need to push about expression because in the case of most dancers – if they do the dance fully – it becomes in itself interesting to watch. If you don't make demands as a spectator but you really look, you find that most things are interesting. There's the other side of it, of course. If you have certain fixed expectations, then you look for those and miss something else.

(Cunningham, 1985: 153)

At the same time, it is well known historically that certain choreographers have tended to work regularly with dancers who inspire them, and much has been written about one of Cunningham's most valued collaborators, Carolyn Brown.

In addition to being a superb technical dancer with elegant bearing and precisely articulated gestures, she also has an excellent visual memory and has functioned as the *régisseuse* of the company during her association with it ... she has always been his most resilient and compliant dancer in picking up on his choreographic suggestions and fleshing them out to his satisfaction.

(McDonagh, 1973 in Kostelanetz, 1992: 5)

For Balanchine, the impetus to create ballets was derived from endless interest in the ways that the classically trained female body can move, which presented him with continuous challenges. McDonagh (1983: 15–16) writes that Balanchine's all-consuming interest in making ballets for female bodies tended to destabilize his relationships with the women themselves. He was married to at least four ballerinas – Tamara Geva, Vera Zorina, Maria Tallchief and Tanaquil LeClercq – and continued to be inspired by his muses Suzanne Farrell, Merrill Ashley and Gelsey Kirkland.

Like Balanchine, many choreographers are inspired both by their dancers and by the music of particular composers. Jiri Kylian was stimulated by the music of many classical composers such as Stravinsky, Mozart, Vivaldi and Janacek, and Frederick Ashton, Richard Alston and Mark Morris all seem to have acknowledged music as the muse for much of their respective bodies of work.

Dancers involved in the creative process of making a new work are also making an investment. They need to feel that they are valued, that they are contributing to something worthwhile which will augment their personal growth as artists. When David Nixon, Artistic Director of Northern Ballet (based in Leeds, UK), started working on *Cleopatra* (2011), he chose Martha Leebolt as his muse. Martha is a Californian who danced at BalletMet Columbus and later joined Northern Ballet in 2001 where she has become a strong, highly physical and eloquent performer. For several months during 2010 she worked with Nixon and two partners, Tobias Batley and Kenneth Tindall, to develop the material of the major pas de deux which highlight the power and sexuality of her character. These duets also help structure the work in chronological order: Cleopatra with her brother Ptolemy, with Caesar, with Mark Antony, and with Wadget, the god of the Pharaohs.

What provided the catalyst for Nixon to choreograph this work, and what was his starting point for the creation of the character of Cleopatra? In interview he suggests that the subject had been in the back of his mind for some years, but that only when he persuaded Claude-Michel Schonberg to write the score could he proceed:

> I'm portraying Cleopatra as a woman, a queen, a mother, a lover. I want the audience to understand her as a human as much as someone going to lead a country. She possessed a quality that could engage men and hold them, and I'm hoping to somehow create that kind of charisma, and at the same time let the audience know this was a woman who had children, who was trying to protect them. This was a woman who thought several times in her life that she had achieved her goal only to be left running for her life. There's an incredible woman in there.
>
> When you are creating dance you have to find a reason why a story will work in dance as opposed to just any other medium. Cleopatra is about sensuality and relationships, manipulation and political manoeuvring and these are all things that dance can portray very well.

(www.northernballet.com)

Nixon's choice of casting was totally justified. The critical reviews opined:

> Chief among *Cleopatra*'s assets is its lead. Martha Leebolt won a National Dance Award in 2010 and it is easy to see why: she is a wonderfully eloquent, intelligent performer, who tackles her role with complete assurance.
>
> (www.telegraph.co.uk/culture/theatre/dance/8351914/
> cleopatra-Northern-Ballet-Leeds-Grand-Theatre-
> review.html)

> David Nixon's new ballet about the Serpent of the Nile provides a perfect role for the newly-crowned queen of classical ballet, Martha Leebolt. Any doubts about her Critics' Circle award will be silenced by her performance as the god/queen who bestrides the worlds of semi-divinity and human fallibility like a colossus ... it is Leebolt's performance that keeps the attention. Her fabulously-muscled legs and sexual energy propel the piece through the holes in the music with a reckless, abandoned momentum that is wholly appropriate.
>
> (www.thestage.co.uk/reviews/review.php/31426/cleopatra)

When asked what this experience of creating a new work has meant to her, Martha acknowledged that 'Having a role created on you is an experience that is hard to put into words. Working with David on Cleopatra has unquestionably been the most meaningful and special time of my career.'

PREPARING FOR PERFORMANCE

Nijinsky's sister Bronislava, in her book *Early Memoirs*, gives very detailed accounts of her brother's performances and how he prepared for them:

> She tells how his daily practice was geared towards developing his strength and that he would practise much more difficult feats than were needed for his roles. She also says that he would practise to minimise the preparations for jumps, and

that he worked at finding how to land softly afterwards, so that when he was on stage his performance would appear effortless and flowing.

(Burt, 2010: 220)

Burt quotes Alexandre Benois, for whom Nijinsky was someone who only came alive on stage: 'Having put on his costume, he gradually began to change into another being, the one he saw in the mirror.... The fact that Nijinsky's metamorphosis was predominantly subconscious is in my opinion the very proof of his genius' (Benois, 1941: 289).

The recent film *Black Swan* starring Natalie Portman (as a ballerina who gets chosen to dance the twin roles of Odette–Odile in *Swan Lake*) has certainly given a new perspective to the question: How do dancers prepare themselves for performance, physically and psychologically? But apart from doing a class, and reliving significant moments in the creative process, what methods do dancers employ? Actors might do many of the exercises that Stanislavsky, Brecht or Artaud employed, or do a group activity on stage to get focused. Musicians might meditate, or play through the whole piece without playing. Dancers might dance through the whole thing without dancing, through kinaesthetic sensation, before they go on stage. They might concentrate on the characterization of a role, or the sensory feeling of an abstract work, or go on stage before curtain up to practise some technically complex part of the choreography.

The writing of Mary Wigman (as edited by Walter Sorell) provides insights not only into her choreographic intentions, but also into the sensory feelings that she experienced *while* dancing. In 1930, Wigman choreographed *Totenmal* to a poem by Albert Talhoff:

> The poetic diction of this work is in itself rhythm and movement in the choreographic sense. More important still, the structure and the contents of the poem give the dancer access to this proper and original field of expression....
>
> She jumps because she wants to fly, battling during the leap with gravity and lightness, overcoming the one to be conquered by the other. Every leap is a battle.

Desire upward toward lightness and light: the law down-
ward toward darkness and heaviness. She does not let go of her
desire. Fighting gravity makes her strong when it is a question
of flying. Overcoming something makes the laughter lighter,
the breathing happier. She pulls away from the ground, throws
herself into the air, defiantly and without fear: she floats, flies
between heaven and earth for a short moment.

(1984: 116, 19–20)

All these examples of how professional dancers have approached the
preparation for performance can be useful tools for students but
arguably there is no substitute for personal experience. A Dance
Studies student may well harbour dreams of becoming a professional
dancer, and will need to develop his or her personal approaches to
how to prepare for a role, interpret a character, establish a persona
or communicate feeling to an audience. It is perhaps dangerous to
imagine that there are any hard and fast methods for becoming a
truly expressive, interpretative dancer, but the qualities of curiosity,
thoughtfulness, intelligence, imagination, truthfulness and honesty
in the studio and on stage can surely contribute to a worthwhile
performance.

VIEWING PERFORMANCES

We can also learn much as performers from viewing the performances of others, from being inspired by the experience of being
engaged in a performance as a spectator. Audience members have
different motivations for and expectations of going to watch performance; they might admire the virtuosity of physicality of the
performer, or feel some sympathy for the character being played.
Perhaps the performance evokes personal memories or solicits an
objective evaluation. For some, there will be a sense or kinaesthetic
empathy, where you are sitting still in the theatre feeling as if you
are truly participating in the dance on stage.

Further insights are gleaned by reading texts which analyse the
making of a work, and by reading dance criticism. Lorna Sanders
has written a number of resource books for teachers and students of
dance, the third based on the work of the Henry Oguike Dance
Company. Here is an example of critical writing from Judith

Mackrell, describing Henri Oguike's work *Front Line* (2002), choreographed to Shostakovich's Ninth String Quartet:

> His signature work, *Front Line*, is ... organised around fierce, linear tracks of movement. As the six ... dancers spread out in stamping single file, their percussive moves unequivocally beat out the music's violent rhythms. Yet what we register ... is the confined area in which the dancers move, the sense that their collective frenzy is beating against invisible walls. You don't have to know the history of Shostakovich's struggle with the Soviet authorities to feel the howl of claustrophobia embodied in the music.
>
> (Sanders, 2004: 37)

Wayne McGregor's ballet *Infra* (2008) for the Royal Ballet was so eloquently described by Sarah Compton that her review evokes a real sense of being present in the theatre:

> To Max Richter's mournful score, 12 outstanding dancers meet and part, whisper to one another, pause and move on. Their movements show all McGregor's characteristic invention: legs scissored, backs and arms arched, articulations extreme and entwined. There is a mood of mystery; sometimes the gestures recall a half-forgotten human action; the moods switch from impassioned to enraged in a split second.
>
> With the simplest and most economical of means, McGregor conjures the seething life of a city, the sense of constant change. In the programme he quotes TS Eliot's 'The Waste Land': 'I had not thought death had undone so many', and there is a sense in which these bodies are also shades, the things that lie beneath.
>
> In one heart–stopping moment, a great crowd of real people in street clothes burst onto the stage, and walk unseeing past Lauren Cuthbertson, spotlit in a wail of collapsing agony. At another, six couples engage in six slithering, complex duets in six parallel squares of light, like a frieze of life, their physical conversations passing from one to the other at quicksilver speed.
>
> (Compton, 2008)

For the Dance Studies student, critical writings about dance are generally a valuable resource from a number of perspectives: for reading descriptors of works that have not been seen or are not available digitally; for discovering what has been said in terms of interpretation or evaluation; and thirdly, for learning more about *how* to write about dance, to be an effective communicator about the work rather than simply be opinionated about its quality. Whether or not a review is positive or negative, students can engage with the sentiment being expressed, interrogate the view and question how it is articulated, generally improving their own critical writing in the process.

Going to the theatre for the live experience of viewing theatrical dance is essential for a dance student. From a personal perspective, for much of my life going to the theatre was the only way of seeing dance performed by professional dancers. As a lecturer in Dance at Bretton Hall, I drove the college minibus all over Yorkshire and Lancashire in order to transport students to see a range of choreographic performances in Bradford and Leeds, Sheffield and Manchester, and I also initiated annual trips to London's Dance Umbrella. Having acquired a video recorder in 1980, I started to collect hundreds of VHS tapes of everything to do with dance and performance that could be copied 'off air' from television in order to have resources for my dance history lectures or choreography exemplars. We started files of newspaper cuttings to supplement the lack of dance books and other resources. Today, 30 years later, numerous books on dance are published annually, and thanks to online resources, youtube and thousands of dance-related websites, it is possible to view clips of choreographies from all over the world, in every genre and style, and from every context. These resources are of inestimable value to dance students, though they cannot take the place of experiencing a wide range of live performances.

RESOURCES FOR PERFORMANCE

Today, students are very privileged to be able to source such insights and inspiration about performance via the web, though the most comprehensive belong to the major companies which can afford such sophisticated and accessible sites.

Generally, dance companies are now well aware of the great interest that audiences have in seeing what happens 'back stage' – in the training of the dancers, in the process of making choreography and the intentions of artistic directors, in how sets and costumes are designed and created, *and* in the creative and experiential development of roles. From the website of the Royal Ballet in London, we can view dozens of video clips detailing choreographers talking about the objectives behind new productions, composers and scenographers explaining artistic decisions on music, sets and costumes, and dancers explaining and demonstrating how to make a role their own.

On the website of Nederlands Dans Theater at the time of writing are 136 video clips of choreographic works ready to view; it is fascinating, for example, to see two works by Jiri Kylian, former Artistic Director. His work *Forgotten Land* (1981, music by Benjamin Britten) was reconstructed for the 2011 season, and shared a programme with his latest work, *Mémoires d'oubliettes* (2009, music by Dirk Haubrich). One can recognize the characteristic features of his choreography, but also note subtle changes in his dance style, in the choreographic devices that are utilized, in performer intensity (www.ndt.nl).

Equally, on the website of the New York City Ballet one can find The Viewing Room, which allows students and the general public to learn much more about specific works through extended interviews with dancers and extended video clips of the works from the repertoire (www.nycballet.com/company/viewing.html).

Another phenomenon began recently: the screening of major works from opera houses and dance companies in cinemas all over the world. On 6 March 2011, for example, I attended a cinema in Malta, in the Mediterranean, to see a production of *Don Quixote* from the Bolshoi Ballet in Moscow, broadcast in real time to over 300 cinemas in 22 countries. The choreography by Petipa/Gorsky has been adapted in a new choreographic version by Alexei Fadeyechev and sets by Sergei Barkhin. Kitri/Dulcinea was danced by Natalia Osipova, with Ivan Vasiliev as Balilio, Alexei Loparevich as Don Quixote, and Alexander Petukhov as Sancho Panza. I also saw Nicolas Le Riche's production of *Caligula* (2005) at the same cinema, streamed direct from the Paris Opéra Ballet.

These opportunities are a wonderful resource, not simply for all undergraduate students of Dance and dancers in training but for members of the general public to experience performances of high quality.

FURTHER READING

Franklin, E. (1996) *Dance Imagery for Technique and Performance* Champaign, Ill.: Human Kinetics

Nagrin, D. (1997) *The Six Questions: Acting Technique for Dance Performance* Pittsburgh, Pa.: University of Pittsburgh Press

APPRECIATING DANCE

When we go to the theatre as spectators to see a dance performance, a number of very interesting things are happening simultaneously. We watch a dance that has been made by a choreographer, sometimes in collaboration with dancers or with other artists such as composers and designers. The dance has been worked out on the bodies of dancers who also contribute to its interpretation and meaning. These dancers perform the dance; we sit in the audience, 'reading' the dance, responding to what we see, bringing our own senses, interpretations and translations. And typically, each member of the audience may well have a personal response to what has been seen, depending on elements like age, gender, class, culture and experience of watching dances.

For the lay person, the idea that, in Dance Studies, we learn to 'appreciate' dance will probably be taken to mean that we respond to a performance of a choreographic work favourably, dependent upon our own likes, tendencies and aesthetic preferences. Often this means that dance aficionados will only go to see the works that they enjoy, know something about, and have a taste for: for example, people who support various ballet companies around the world as patrons or 'friends'; or those who prefer commercial dance of the genre found in musical theatre or television variety shows. Others respond to the marketing strategies of theatres or visiting companies, attracted by the imagery of the photographs or the written descriptions of the dances to be performed.

But those who choose to be students of Dance in higher education will be introduced to all kinds of new works that challenge their perceptions – including dances with no music, dances with no

theme, and dances with no dance steps. For the advantage of studying the subject in depth is to engage with a *wide* range of dance
works, from both well-established and new companies, from inside
our own culture and from way beyond it, to become knowledgeable
and to develop expertise of theories and practical application of the
discipline. In doing so, we usually open up new territory, develop
intellectual autonomy – or the ability to think for ourselves – and are
able to appreciate, analyse and evaluate in more rational ways. In
addition, far more resources are now available to support the quest.
The work of many choreographers is available on video, DVD,
youtube, and the websites of most major dance companies in the
world. In addition, recent developments in technology on digital
archiving allow us to view and analyse a whole range of choreographic approaches; two good examples are the work of William
Forsythe on the Synchronous Objects website, and the Siobhan
Davies Archive, Replay (see References, pp. 203–4).

Students studying Dance at college and university level will be
involved in practical and theoretical sessions which introduce them
to various methods of analysing the making, performing and appreciating of the art form of dance in a number of contexts. This
chapter details how students begin to develop their conceptual
understandings and their skills of verbalizing, discussing, writing
and presenting in several ways. Not only do we investigate the
history and aesthetics of our own discipline, but increasingly we
have recognized the need to investigate dance in its socio-cultural
context. Just as we cannot fully understand the baroque dance
forms of Versailles in the reign of Louis XIV without knowledge
of the national and political beliefs of the period, neither should we
study contemporary dance works without developing an awareness
of a range of different theoretical perspectives which can help us to
illuminate meaning-making. These include ideas from classicism,
modernism and post-modernism, and theories from other disciplines like theatre studies, anthropology, ethnography, semiotics,
phenomenology, cultural studies, feminism/gender studies, race/
ethnicity, politics and inter-culturalism. Often, these fields overlap
and interact. The best way to describe this idea of *looking at a dance
from different perspectives* is to imagine that you wear a different pair
of glasses, perhaps with a different colour of lens, each time you
approach a different perspective.

For example, if we read Curtis M. Wong's review of Mark Morris's *The Hard Nut* (1991) performed on its thirtieth anniversary, what do we learn about this work?

Nutcracker, Interrupted: Mark Morris' *The Hard Nut* is a Delightfully Zany Take on the Beloved Holiday Ballet

From the moment the curtain rises onto a pack of booze-swilling suburbanites engaged in a libidinous promenade, it's clear *The Hard Nut* is not your ordinary *Nutcracker*.

To be fair, the Mark Morris Dance Group's modern take on the yuletide ballet – which returns to the Brooklyn Academy of Music (BAM) through Dec. 19 – includes many familiar scenes: a young girl receives a nutcracker on Christmas Eve, and her pine-jawed plaything morphs into a brawny, flesh-and-blood hunk before the pair waltzes off into a magical kingdom of snowflakes and sugar plums.

But choreographer Morris has cleverly transplanted the tale from its traditional European setting to a pop-art version of '60s and '70s U.S. suburbia, complete with Formica furniture, G.I. Joe action figures and even a Barbie doll dream house. Though updating such a revered holiday classic is undoubtedly risky … *The Hard Nut* strips the ballet of much of its saccharine excess, and successfully incorporates much of the darkness found in E.T.A. Hoffmann's 1816 tale on which Pyotr Ilyich Tchaikovsky based his most beloved work.

Morris conceived of *The Hard Nut* during a three-year stint at the Théâtre de la Monnaie in Brussels in 1991, yet the current production – which had its NYC premiere at BAM a year later – has a decidedly American feel, and still looks as lively and energetic as ever. Much has been made of Morris' decision to cast dancers of the opposite gender in many prominent roles (including the heroine's mother), but the end result is far from camp. As both Mrs. Stahlbaum and the Queen, John Heginbotham is completely convincing, while Kraig Patterson has the daunting task of being one of the few cast members to spend the entire show *en pointe* as the family maid. And many will be surprised to learn that the mischievous tween brother Fritz is played by June Omura, one of the company's original cast members.

Many of the ensemble numbers play further with both gender roles and the story's specifics. In a throwback to the original story, the Prince (David Levanthal) is assumed to be the nephew of the delightfully swishy Drosselmeier (William Smith III), who gifts the toy nutcracker to Marie (Lauren Grant) at the story's onset. Nephew and uncle share a tender embrace in an Act I *pas de deux* normally reserved for the Nutcracker Prince and Marie; though the intent is to establish the familial connection rather than anything erotic, the male-on-male visual is nonetheless striking. Typically a stoic number in white tutus, 'Waltz of the Snowflakes' is transformed into a visual tour-de-force comprising performers of both genders. Wearing midriff-baring silver costumes and the headdresses resembling soft-serve ice cream, the dancers create the illusion of a blizzard by tossing handfuls of confetti 'snowflakes' as they swirl, twirl and leap across the stage.

Morris departs most dramatically from the tried-and-true story for much of Act II, which is normally a series of disconnected dance numbers. Here, he introduces a hideously ugly Princess Pirlipat, for whom Drosselmeier must locate a magical hard nut which, once cracked open, will restore her beauty. This provides a much-needed context for the Chinese, Spanish and Russian dance numbers, each a playful pastiche of national stereotypes. Yet what may seem to be an overly elaborate subplot is, once again, a nod to Hoffmann's original book. After an acrobatically sexy 'Waltz of the Flowers,' Marie and the Nutcracker Prince finally do get their grand romantic number in Tchaikovsky's best-known composition, 'Dance of the Sugar Plum Fairy'. Though the heroine normally spends the entirety of the show in a nightgown, she changes into a red dress and doffs her ballet slippers for bare feet as if to emphasize her coming-of-age transition as she lands her man.

The production team also deserves kudos for its stripped-down, almost Brechtian staging. Inspired by the horror-comic art of Charles Burns, Adrianne Lobel's largely black-and-white set resembles a massive camera lens, with banners and props occasionally interjecting onto the proscenium. In contrast, the Martin Paklendinaz costumes are bold, splashy and colorful, from the gaudy red-and-green pantsuits for party guests in Act I to burkas in royal blue donned for the 'Arabian Dance' in the middle of Act II. And Tchaikovsky's score, robustly conducted by Robert Cole, has never sounded better.

Curtis M. Wong, *The Huffington Post*, 13 December, 2010 Content Copyright 2011 Huffington Post.com used with permission.

What do you learn about this version of *The Nutcracker*, and how does it contrast with the Christmas ballet that so many ballet companies put on each December? The review suggests many questions from a cultural perspective: for example, how does setting the ballet in a pop-art 1960s-1970s US suburban context affect your view? What do you think is intended by casting dancers in the opposite gender to that of the character? What sorts of questions could be raised by the fact that the famous pas de deux of the original is danced here by two men? How would you attempt to 'decode' the costumes in terms of their ability to convey meaning? These and other questions will be addressed more deeply later in the chapter.

STARTING POINTS

It is important for Dance students to develop the ability to reflect on the work of others and to reflect on their own choreography. For example, Dance scholars need to be able to write about their own creative processes in an informed way, using language which they can share with others, and detailing all the creative decisions and stages of the dance-making process. They learn to analyse both the processes and the finished dance products of other people, especially of professional choreographers, and to consider the myriad differences in concept, context and methods, as well as genre and style.

For example, imagine watching four different versions of *Swan Lake*: the first might be a version danced by the Kirov Ballet, with the more or less original choreography by Petipa/Ivanov from the 1890s; the second could be a version of the Cullberg Ballet of Sweden, choreographed by Matts Ek in 1987 in a much more contemporary style which seems to totally subvert the 'known' version – Ek's Odette (danced by Ana Laguna) is barefoot, stocky, seemingly bald, Siegfried, the Prince, is dominated by his mother, and the cygnets are awkward and gauche. The third *Swan Lake* is an all-male version by Matthew Bourne which was danced by Adventures in Motion Pictures in London in 1995, with the Odette/Odile roles performed by Adam Cooper of the Royal Ballet; and in the fourth, *Birdbrain* by Garry Stewart, made for the Australian Dance Theatre in 2001, he seemed to pull apart and deconstruct various elements of *Swan Lake* and reconstruct it in a 'high-energy mix of ballet, 1980s-style Eurocrash, hip-hop, yoga, acrobatics and breakdance' (Midgelow, 2007: 67–8).

We might ask what kinds of words, and what frameworks for analysis, might be helpful in describing each of these four versions, as they are all so radically different. We would need to approach these four choreographies with distinct analytical tools, to be aware of how and why these versions came about; we do this by raising questions about the style and construction of the choreography, of the particular aesthetic, and in particular by asking questions to do with historical, cultural and socio-political concerns.

But to start at the beginning: in Dance Studies, students will probably start the course by learning to identify all the components of a dance. How many dancers are there? What is the style of the dance, and what skills do the dancers need? What steps are used, and where does the dance travel in space? In identifying such elements as the dancers, the physical setting, the music or accompaniment, the movement or dance language, the choreographic development, devices and structures, we learn to describe what the dance looks like and what its ingredients are. We might learn to use the theories of Rudolf Laban (body, dynamic, spatial features and relationships), or the components illustrated by Janet Adshead and others in *Dance Analysis: Theory and Practice* (1988) – movement, spatial elements, dynamic elements, dancers, visual setting, aural elements and complexes – which signals elements very noticeable or specific to the particular dance. Authors like Bartenieff and Lewis (1980) and Hanna (1979) offer slightly different models for component analysis. Understanding matters of structure and relationship are also important for the appreciation of a dance: this means understanding not simply the macro-structure of the whole dance but the construction of steps, phrases, sections, the nexus of patterns, repeated movements, variation and canon as they portray the relationships of the dancers; also the progression and the high points or climaxes of the dance. Students of Dance certainly learn much about how to identify or utilize these *ingredients* of a dance, but this kind of formal analysis does little to tell us what the dance *means*.

Next, therefore, students might be asked about the meaning of the dance. How do they interpret it? Does it have a story, theme, plot and identifiable characters, with clear relationships and a specific meaning? Is it therefore quite easy to interpret, as perhaps the whole class will offer similar ideas? On the other hand, is the dance difficult to interpret because it seems so abstract, or because it is so layered and could have many meanings? ... How does it fire your imagination, and what does it make you think or feel?

Pauline Hodgens's chapter in Adshead (1988) discusses not only the concepts through which interpretations are made – i.e. four elements of socio-cultural background, that is context, genre, style, and subject matter, but also concepts relating to the interpretation of a specific dance – i.e. character, qualities and meanings/ significances:

> interpreting combines the skills of *noticing, seeing* and *discerning* with those of *recognising, characterising* and *making sense of* the object or event in question. The process of interpreting includes the discerning of the features and form and the recognition of *character* and *qualities*. Interpreting is the process for discovering or revealing the *meaning* of certain objects or events.
>
> (Hodgens in Adshead, 1988: 61)

When we watch a dance, we tend to respond to what we see by relating it to what we already know. Does it relate to any theatre dance we have seen before? Or does the theme seem somehow familiar, resonant of a novel that you have read or a play or a film that you have seen? Perhaps the dance explores relationships that you have experienced yourself in your home life or socially, or is it simply that the dance reawakens memories or images that are meaningful to you?

When students are asked to evaluate a dance, they are actually being asked to value it. If we can understand the subject matter and also appreciate the skill, dexterity or virtuosity of the dance ... do we like it better than a piece which is very complex or sophisticated? When we describe, analyse, interpret or evaluate dances, we learn, understand and use new kinds of language which are appropriate to the academic study of our discipline. It is not enough to say 'I like it'. We need to be able to explain what we liked or disliked about it and why.

DANCE AESTHETICS

Another method of analysing dance focuses on aesthetic categories – beauty, judgement, taste, imagination – whatever it is that is pleasing or displeasing to the senses. Here, a brief overview of the theories of art, from Aristotle to the late twentieth century, includes notions of imitation, beauty, expression and form.

What is 'the aesthetic'? And how does it relate to art? What makes something aesthetically pleasing, and how can we experience something aesthetically pleasing? In other words, why bother with art?

> Here are some of the things that people do in their spare time: they read novels, they read poetry, they go to the theatre, they listen to music, they go to art exhibitions, they make trips to look at buildings or to view scenery. These are all aesthetic activities. People engage in them from choice and for their own sake. Reading a novel will not help me earn my living (unless I am a professional reviewer or a teacher of literature). Going to an art exhibition will not cure me of any physical ailment. A visit to a beauty spot will not make my house any warmer. Why then do people seek out aesthetic experiences? One obvious answer would be that people do these things because they enjoy them. It gives us pleasure to read books or to go to the theatre, to listen to music or look at paintings, to gaze at fine buildings or contemplate the beauties of nature. This answer tells us something, but not very much. Why seek this particular kind of pleasure? ... [What] makes these particular activities worthwhile? There are many ways of getting pleasure: having a drink or going for a brisk walk may be pleasurable too. Why bother about art or about natural beauty? Why spend time, money and effort on these particular sources of pleasure? Is there something special about aesthetic

experiences which make them pleasurable in some special way? Is there any further point to them, apart from the pleasure they afford us?

(Sheppard, 1987: 1)

Questions:

1 What kinds of feelings do you gain from art?
2 What things in nature can produce similar feelings?
3 What dance pieces have brought about feelings like this?
4 What is your taste?
5 Thus what do you dislike and why?
6 How do you think this personal aesthetic has been developed?

Jerome Stolnitz (1960: 32–42) argues that we tend to perceive the world selectively, concentrating on some features and ignoring others, depending on our purpose. This he calls 'the attitude of *practical* perception'. But on occasion we pay attention to a thing simply for the sake of enjoying the way it looks or sounds or feels. This is the *aesthetic* attitude of perception. Stolnitz defines this as 'disinterested and sympathetic attention to and contemplation of any object of awareness whatever, for its own sake alone'.

If we consider the stages through which a work of art passes, we find that at each stage, aesthetic is important:

1 making (conceptualizing, imagining, intuiting)
2 presenting
3 audience response (feeling, senses, imagination)
4 evaluation (intellectual formulation of aesthetic response – awareness of artistic convention, of inherited traditions and contemporary practices, as well as a knowledge of critical commentaries).

Aesthetic derives from the Greek word meaning 'through the senses'. It refers to the matrix of sense, feeling and sensibility, i.e. a form of intelligence:

Through aesthetic intelligence we are able to apprehend a realm of meaning and value essential to any full concept of human existence. In the development of understanding the aesthetic mode is as important as the discursive mode, and it is the arts which develop sensuous intelligence for by this very nature they work through it and on it in both their creation and their reception.

(Abbs in Pateman, 1991: 8)

In 1931, Herbert Read wrote that

all artists have this same intention, the desire to please; and art is most simply and most usually defined as an attempt to create pleasing forms. Such forms satisfy our sense of beauty and the sense of beauty is satisfied when we are able to appreciate a unity or harmony of formal relations amongst our sense-perceptions.

However, it is a misconception to assume that all that is art is beautiful, and all that is beautiful is art.

The concept of beauty arose in ancient Greece, where art, as well as religion, was an idealization of nature, and especially of man as the culminating point of the process of nature. This type of beauty was inherited by Rome, and revived at the Renaissance. 'A thing of beauty is a joy for ever' suggests that beauty in an object is timelessly recognizable: but 'beauty is in the eye of the beholder' suggests that what is picked out as beautiful will vary from person to person, period to period, culture to culture. Arguably, we cannot specify those things that will always *please through the senses*. Despite our knowledge of classical rules for composition – line, balance, perspective, harmony, unity – or the golden section, designed to ensure proportion in drawing or sculpting the human body – artists no longer use and fit pre-existing rules.

AN AESTHETIC SENSE/TASTE

There is an assumption that individuals can develop an aesthetic sense or taste, and further, that, by consensus, a right and wrong about standards and taste develop through hegemony.

What is hegemony?

Gramsci's theory of hegemony refers to a situation in which an alliance of certain social groups can exert 'total social authority' over other subordinate groups, not simply by coercion or by the direct imposition of ideas, but by 'winning and shaping consent so that the power of the dominant classes appears both legitimate and natural'.

(Hall, 1977: 339)

But who, in our domain, has this power? It is fairly evident that parents, teachers, lecturers, critics, directors of companies, museums or galleries – all these people may have some influence on setting our standards of taste at particular times of our lives.

Aesthetic appreciation may be directed at a variety of natural or man-made objects, perceived by any of the five senses. But we must understand ourselves and our own psychology to understand our own individual responses: to food, landscapes, clothes, people, etc. How can we explain to others why we feel that something or someone is aesthetically beautiful? How do we make aesthetic judgements? Historically, three main types of theory have been proposed (at different periods of time) as the distinguishing feature of art: imitation, expression and form.

Imitation – art reflecting reality, works of art appearing to imitate or represent things in the real world (figurative work – mimetic work – classical and neo-classical, naturalism (see Plato's *Republic* Book X, Aristotle's *Poetics*).

The Platonic view not only offers a perspective on what sort of thing a work of art is but also places a value on it. But if works of art appear to imitate or represent, they could equally be copies or fakes, and in any case, do we assess success in art in terms of how well they imitate? The term 'mimesis' is often translated as 'representational' which gets away from the evaluative implications of the word 'imitation' and makes the aesthetic context clear – a relationship between world/art and copy/model.

Expression – an emotion expressed (as intended by the artist?) which may or may not be triggered in the audience. This theory started with Tolstoy in *What is Art?* (translated Maude, 1898; www. archive.org/details/tolstoyonart00tolsuoff) which argues that art is the contagion of feeling: he says that the true artist both expresses and evokes emotion. This is a very simplistic view, and over-emphasizes the irrational aspects of our response to art. In the romanticism of the nineteenth century, ideals of originality, creative imagination and depth of feeling were embraced, for example by the poet Wordsworth who said 'Poetry is the spontaneous overflow of powerful feeling'.

More sophisticated theories of art as expression were put forward by Benedetto Croce in his book *Aesthetic* (translated Ainslie, 1922) and Collingwood in *The Principles of Art* (1938). Both Croce and Collingwood made a fundamental distinction between conceptual thought and intuition (Croce) or imagination (Collingwood). That is, first the artist receives the raw data of sensation and perception, then he feels emotions (without necessarily being conscious of them), then he expresses them imaginatively – that is, the concept is formulated. Both philosophers, having defined art in this way, then treat expression as providing a criterion by which works of art may be evaluated – what is not expressive is not art. Both condemn entertainment and religious or patriotic art, and both concentrate on the activity of the artist rather than the response of the audience.

The weakness of this theory of art is that it neglects differences between the arts, differences of response or critical vocabulary. It also concentrates too much on what might be going on in the mind of the artist, and does little justice to the intellectual elements or the craft in art. Expression is arguably only one element of art. And how do we identify expression in abstract art?

Susanne Langer in *Feeling and Form* (1953) recognizes that form cannot ultimately be separated from expression:

> A work of art is intrinsically expressive; it is designed to abstract and present forms for perception – forms of life and feeling, activity, suffering, selfhood – whereby we conceive of these realities, which otherwise we can but blindly undergo. Every good work of art is beautiful; as soon as we find it so, we have grasped its expressiveness, and until we do we have not seen it as good art, though we may have ample intellectual reason to

believe that it is so. Beautiful works may contain elements that, taken in isolation, are hideous.... The emergent form, the whole, is alive and therefore beautiful, as awful things may be – as gargoyles, and fearful African masks, and the Greek tragedies of incest and murder are beautiful. Beauty is not identical with the normal, and certainly not with charm and sense appeal, though all such properties may go to the making of it. Beauty is expressive form.

(Langer, 1953: 395–396)

Form – the shape, arrangement of parts, the visible aspect, the principle by which the work of art coheres (for example, the pyramid forms of baroque art, the three-act ballet or the five-act play). This third general type of theory about art considers that the essence of art is to be found in form: a search for details of formal features in a work of art, its form and structure, its micro- and macro-form.

- Music: formal features are most important and most readily perceived (e.g. verse, chorus; theme and variations; major/minor sections; etc.).
- Visual arts: proportion, balance and symmetry and important aspects (e.g. Greek sculpture of the classical period; Renaissance painting).
- Literature: formal features include metre and rhythm in poetry; interweaving of plot and sub-plots in novels or plays (e.g. the three plays which make up Aeschylus' *Oresteia* are all concerned with justice, and the presentation of this theme from different points of view shapes the trilogy and gives it coherence).

The weakness in this aesthetic theory is that it ignores the expressive, and concentrates on the formal elements alone. Roger Fry (1926) and Clive Bell (1914) both write about the importance of 'significant form' but never really explain what sort of form counts as significant. Both talk of a 'special aesthetic emotion' aroused by the perception of significant form but do not define or analyse it: significant of what? Can formal features of visual art be considered in isolation? Of course, as students we need to attempt to analyse the differences: 'A comprehensive formalist theory which applied to all the arts would be one which saw the essential characteristic of art in its presentation of elements in ordered and unified relationships' (Sheppard 1987: 52).

Unlike the other two theories, formalism tends to be concerned solely with the art work itself, and offers no account of the relationship of the work to its maker or its audience.

It is evident that none of these three philosophical theories can do justice to the diversity of all types of art; they can, however, be useful in understanding differences in approach to the conception and making of art (from an artist's point of view) and the reception of art (from an audience point of view). And as people involved in performance, interested in questions about judgement, taste and beauty, how can we apply them to our own ways of conceptualizing and making performance or dance? How can we use them to help us appreciate the work of others, and to understand our personal responses to new work?

DANCE CRITICISM

Dance critics write for newspapers and magazines every day. Sally Banes (1994) gives us a clear exposé of the kinds of critical writing we can expect to find in them in her essay 'On your Fingertips: Writing Dance Criticism' by detailing the operations that a critic can perform:

- Description: what the dancers did – what does the work look and feel like?
- Interpretation: what they communicated – what does the dance mean?
- Evaluation: how remarkable it was – is the work good?
- Contextualization: where does the work come from aesthetically and/or historically?

Banes gives some examples of these operations, singly and in more complex combinations; she identifies 15 possibilities of critical writing and demonstrates many of them. She specifies the critic's job as threefold: to complete the work in the reader's understanding; to unfold the work in an extended time and space after the performance; and to enrich the experience of the work. One fascinating factor is the evident confidence of writers like Théophile Gautier, who writes fairly judgemental criticism with personal comment about certain dancers: e.g. 'Mme Guy-Stéphan exhibits as natural talent an extraordinary lightness; she bounds up like a rubber ball and comes down like a feather or a snow flake' (1853, in Cohen, 1974). There is little description of the choreography of the ballet, but much of this performer. By contrast, Banes (1994: 43) notes a shift in critical values by the end of the twentieth century, speaking about a 'sense of anxiety of aesthetic evaluation' in a world of political correctness, when artists and critics themselves challenge the 'right' of the critic to judge a work created by someone outside her 'race'/ethnicity/class/gender/etc.

In academic courses the demands for writing critiques and evaluations are not so complex initially. For example, in the first year of a course of study you might be asked to analyse a piece of choreography *formally*: as objectively as possible you identify the components of the dance and note the relationship of elements to the whole work; a formalist approach tends to preclude interpretations. Or you may be asked to *interpret* the dance from your own perspective, which allows you to be much more subjective, and give your own opinion, as long as you also express your reasons for it.

Example of a formal analysis

The dance begins with an imposing movement sequence performed on a diagonal travelling towards the audience. This is accompanied by an orchestral instrumental piece of traditional music, bringing a powerful and dramatic quality into the composition. The choreography is thoroughly driven by the dominant structure of the music and leaves little space for interpretation or alternative approaches of musicality and rhythm.

After the beginning sequence the dancer primarily remains in the centre of the stage, performing several short linear pathways and static positions leading into a more circular use of the space. The piece culminates with a sequence of spatial spirals and a fixed finishing position. Throughout the performance the dancer maintains a frontal direction and focus, clearly intending to show a rehearsed piece of dance to an audience. The focus is both concentrated and graceful while partly straining the performer to use his breath as an additional tool to deepen and clarify the movement material.

Example of interpretative analysis

Sally performed a particularly expressive and self-reflecting solo. From the moment of her strong entrance she invited me to experience the (his)story of her own body and the different processes and changes it has passed through. The dance shows how her physique and her body awareness have changed from adolescence to womanhood and motherhood. The performer recreates the internal experience of this development and physically illustrates it through very refined and researched movement.

In the beginning of the piece the posture of the dancer is introverted and doubtful. She even draws back into the wings after first stepping on stage. Throughout the solo this initial inhibition develops into a more confident physical alignment allowing stronger impulses to take over the movement. The transformation is also noticeable in Sally's facial expressions which accompany the movement and are integral to the external and internal processes of the dance. Towards the end of the solo the performer repeatedly moves from the hips and pulls her own hair, introducing a range of dynamics and tension as well as dramatic sensitivity.

The movement is carried by a strong instrumental piece of music and reverberates the impulses of the sound. The dancer's body gets drawn into the resonance and reflects it back towards the audience. Through this process Sally enabled me to take an intimate look at her inner self and I found myself drawn into a world of empowering femininity and marking experiences. I could physically feel the sensation of struggle, transformation, shame and relief. The contorted performance style created an atmosphere of both obscurity and familiarity and encouraged me to reflect on my personal bodily development as a woman and as a dancer.

By analysing the dance work of other members of the group, our peers, in these two distinct ways, we can identify two very distinct perspectives which require us to develop two different kinds of skills, the *descriptive* and the *interpretative*: first, the ability to recognize separate elements in one dance: what is the body doing, where does it move on stage, what kind of qualities of speed, weight and flow can be noted, what is the interaction between performers, etc.? the second, we are concerned with the response of the 'reader' of the work: what does it feel like and how can I make sense of this work? What does it mean to me, and why?

CONSIDERATION OF DIFFERENCES IN CONCEPT, CONTEXT AND METHODS

Chapter 2 above considered the various stages of making a dance. In appreciating and analysing dances, in addition to examining the content and form of a dance, we may be guided by our understandings of composition and choreography when we consider the differences between concepts, contexts and methods. For example, in analysing a piece by Trisha Brown, the American post-modern choreographer, it would be helpful to ascertain what her intentions were, how she made the work, and whether or not we should consider any particular context. Sanjoy Roy wrote about the Trisha Brown Dance Company's performances for Dance Umbrella in London in November 2010:

> Over a weekend of performances, installations, filmed interviews and archive footage, you could track Brown's wayward path from youthful radical to art-house figurehead. She began by stripping dance of everything she could, just to see what was left. First to go were music and story. 'I did not connect,' she remembers, 'to the redundancy – to the triple redundancy – of a dance which would have a story, about which one was dancing, and a musical score, also about which one was dancing.' Out of the window, too, went codified dance styles (too much theatrical baggage) and, indeed, theatres (ditto). The question then was, having thrown out all this bath water, what to do with the baby she was left holding?

He continues:

> The 'machinery' of dance – how to make something – seems to be Brown's perennial concern. Her early pieces were simple in construction, if not in outcome, like the 'accumulations' in which units of movement accrue one by one so that the choreography looks like an ever-growing molecule. Film footage shows where that simplicity led: in her complex solo Accumulation with Talking Plus Watermotor (1978), Brown cut between two completely different dances, while also telling two different stories. No triple redundancy there.
>
> (www.newstatesman.com)

Here we quickly become aware that Trisha Brown's motivation for making dances is radically different from the issues raised about Mark Morris's *The Hard Nut*. Brown is known as a post-modern choreographer living in New York; she has for more than 40 years been searching for outside organizational patterns to force new methods of construction in her dances: in *Homemade* (1965) she took a series of movements from real life – casting a fishing line, measuring a box, telephoning – and made them minuscule. She strapped a movie projector on her back, and cast images of herself dancing the same dance, as she performed it, which gave the illusion of her dancing body flying round the performance space. In 1968, she began her *Equipment Pieces*, where dancers used various support systems like rope, pulleys and cables to give the illusion of natural movement as they walked down buildings or along walls. Brown was questioning processes of perception of the moving body as it defied gravity and created illusion (Banes, 1987: 80). In 1971 she began making pieces based on mathematical systems of accumulation, in which she created strings of movements accumulated as follows: 1; 1, 2; 1, 2, 3; 1, 2, 3, 4; etc. Here, the audience can easily recognize the building blocks of the movement and discern the form of the dance. And in *Locus* (1975) the genesis of the movement is related to a mathematical system based on an imaginary cube, where at high, medium and low levels letters of the alphabet are assigned to various directions. Dancers write some autobiographical material, 'translate' it into directional instructions, and work out the score in their bodies. This is difficult to describe, but great fun to do (as a Master's student at NYU in the early 1980s, I took a study unit with Brown).

I have described some of Brown's processes in order to point out that, without knowing some of this context and discovering her methods, it would be impossible to write an appropriate analysis of her work. Despite the fact that *Locus* (in performance with several dancers working in close proximity) could be perceived as both expressive and emotional, this audience perception does not relate to Brown's rationale. But it does raise a very important issue in the appreciation of dance; that is, how wide is the gap between what the choreographer intends, and what is received by a member of the audience? And therefore, what do we need to know about how different dances communicate? What kinds of analytical tools might help?

APPLYING SEMIOTICS

Ferdinand de Saussure, a French linguist, first examined how meaning is made by analysing how language uses sounds or written signs to convey ideas. He introduced the idea that the sign is a unit of meaning in language, made up of two parts: a sound or acoustical element called the signifier, and a conceptual element, the signified. He also argued that the relationship between them is arbitrary – that is, there is no connection, intrinsically, between the way a word sounds and the concept to which it refers. For example, in English, we understand the words 'dog' and 'cat' because we have learned what they look and feel like, how they might sound ('woof', 'miaow', etc.). But if we fly to France, the same animals suddenly become *le chien* and *le chat*, and across the border with Germany, *das Hund* and *die Katze*: that is, different words, but the same or similar concept.

Modern sociological thought focused on the social origins of conceptions of the real, the idea that the meaning of the sign is social in origin – and thus our perception of it is coloured by the ways in which our culture manufactures meaning. An artist creates an artefact within a particular society, and it is looked at, analysed and enjoyed by the 'audience' who have the same or different perceptions.

A sign is composed of:

1 a 'signifier' (*signifiant*) = the form which the sign takes (e.g. red rose);
2 the 'signified' (*signifié*) = the concept it represents (e.g. love).

The relationship between the two is *conventional* – that is, it is dependent on social and cultural conventions.

- We make meanings through our creation and interpretation of 'signs'.
- Signs take the form of words, images, sounds, odours, flavours, acts or objects, but such things have no intrinsic meaning and become signs only when we invest them with meaning.

In dance, something similar applies, in that we 'read' a dance by constructing meaning based on the ways in which our society has taught us to shape our actions and perceptions. The meaning of a dance, its signs and symbols, tend to be in layers (see Table 5.1). There may be several different layers, but here they can be conflated in analytical situations. First, there is the meaning that the choreographer invests in the dance during its making: the intention, the motivation for the dance, as we saw in Chapter 2 above. But, second, there are the signs which actually reside in the dance once it is completed, such as the vocabulary, the qualities of movement, the patterns, the context, the dancers themselves. Third, there are the feelings and experiences of the performers as they engage in the making process with the choreographer and then take responsibility for the performance of the dance in the première and beyond; and fourth, the reading of the dance by members of an audience, by different audiences every night. We might ask the question: are they the same thing, or are they four different layers of meaning that might make complete sense and can be used together to explain a dance? Or they are completely arbitrary, possibly unrelated?

And intriguingly, the answer might be yes and it might be no, depending on the particular dance. If a dance has all its elements related, where dance, sound, dancers and space are inextricably interwoven, and where the choreographer has communicated the theme or story clearly to his/her dancers and everyone is 'singing from the same sheet', then it is very possible that the audience (and the critics) will 'get' the intended meaning, more or less. But if the dance is abstract or non-literal, or if the vocabulary was made by indeterminate play of some kind, and if the music was added at the last minute, then it is very unlikely that any two people in the audience will manage to interpret the dance in the same way. Indeed, with an audience of 100, there might be 100 different interpretations.

Table 5.1

The choreographer →	*The dance* →	*The dancers* →	*The audience*
Intention, concept, ideas, content, form	Signs: vocabulary, qualities, patterns	Feelings experiences, interpretation	Reading, perceiving, making sense

If this all sounds too simple, then let us look at some of the codes of communication for further enlightenment.

HOW DO WE COMMUNICATE?

How do you know how your friend is feeling if she doesn't tell you? Can you 'read' her non-verbal messages in her body posture, in her gestures, in particular facial expressions or the way that she walks? We can understand through body language much of what our friends and family are thinking and feeling, by translating their posture: open or closed? Upright or stooped? Tense or relaxed? Focus down towards the floor and inwards, or directly looking at you? But how are we able to read this body language?

Rudolf Laban's investigations of movement style reveal that as any person, any mover, develops skills that are both functional and expressive,

> he/she also develops more specialized body part usage, temporal phrasing, accesses to Space and specific uses for Effort. What is unconscious becomes more conscious. As he/she develops and learns, the mover becomes a more nuanced and effective communicator.... The mover develops a personal 'STYLE'.
>
> (Bradley, 2009: 46)

That is, any movement analyst can recognize the specific personal movement qualities of another individual: the rhythm of a walk, the quality of a gesture, the flow of energy, patterns of small, idiosyncratic gestures like rubbing the nose or sweeping back the hair from the face. Movement is both culturally and personally significant, and each series of movements relates to the context of the mover, her culture, her memories, her intentions or objectives.

Thus, when we know people well, for example family members or friends, we can easily recognize their personal movement style and also something of their feelings through the quality of their movements. Usually, we can tell when they are upset or angry, though we may not know the specific reasons for that state of mind. That is why actors, dancers, anthropologists and others interested in the analysis of human movement will learn how to categorize human movement in terms of four specific components: its bodily actions, its qualities in time, space, weight and flow, its spatial orientation and its relationships (Laban, 1971; Bradley, 2009; Hodgson, 2001).

Laban Movement Analysis is a method for interpreting, describing, visualizing and notating all human movement. It includes the categories Body, Effort, Space, which originated in Laban's own writings, and Shape in some forms (such as the subsequent work of Warren Lamb and Irmgard Bartenieff). As human beings, we understand innately something of these differences; as dancemakers, we use these categories to help us compose dances; as researchers or observers, we can notate and document the specifics of these categories in order to capture and analyse movement in any performance context – theatrical, educational, social and cultural.

The basic concepts of non-verbal communication (NVC), can also be of use to the Dance Studies student. NVC is carried by presentational codes which are limited to face-to-face communication, and can have two functions. First, it conveys information about the speaker through tone of voice, eye movements, posture, gesture, etc. Second, codes can be used to manage the relationship between the speaker and the listener; by using certain gestures, tones of voice or looks, we can communicate in distinct ways. Consider the ways in which a teacher or policeman indicates power, being in charge; how a shop girl shows her willingness to be of service; or how a doctor puts a patient at ease. These codes are used to convey information about the relationship rather than the speaker.

Michael Argyle (1972) published a list of 10 codes transmitted by the human body:

1 bodily contact: whom we touch, and when and where we touch them;
2 proximity: how closely we stand to someone can indicate intimacy or public situations;
3 orientation: how we angle ourselves to others;
4 appearance: height, weight, hair, etc. We can change hair and makeup more easily than weight or height;
5 head nods during personal interaction;
6 facial expression;

7 gestures: some are cultural, or related to emotional states;
8 posture: our ways of standing, sitting, lying can communicate a range of meanings;
9 eye movement and eye contact;
10 non-verbal aspects of speech: both pitch and stress of spoken words, accent, speed, etc.

Again, knowledge of these codes can be utilized by actors or dancers, communications experts or psychologists. Theories of movement analysis that we may be introduced to in Dance Studies may also be of use in educational or teaching contexts, in therapeutic situations, or in ethnographic researching, as in the study of urban dance forms such as hip hop. In early classical ballet, a form of mime or mimetic gesture was used to encode meanings so as to be understood by the audience, for example 'I love you', and the rest of the ballet may have been made of enchaînements or pure sequences of dance. Antony Tudor was one of the first ballet choreographers to use movement to denote real feeling and expression through the choreography and music relationship, as in *Pillars of Fire* (1942) to Arnold Schoenberg's *Verklärte Nacht* ('Transfigured Night'). The music was inspired by a nineteenth-century German poem 'Weib und die Welt' ('Woman and the World'). Set in a time when a child born out of marriage was not condoned by society, the poem is about a pregnant woman who is afraid that her fiancé will not marry her. He, being truly in love with her, accepts the fact that she is carrying someone else's baby, and tells her that the child will be considered his. Tudor's ballet *Pillars of Fire* follows a similar story but with additional characters who help to set up the dramatic situation. He attempts to tell this story, not through mime, but by instilling representational movement into the actual choreography.

Dance uses non-verbal codes all the time – but sometimes audiences find these difficult to read, either because choreographers tend to combine codified vocabulary with mime or because they use representational gestures but then subject them to so much development that they become very symbolic and audiences may not be able to read them effectively. That is, the choreographer transmits a sign or a signal that cannot be read clearly by members of the audience; the lines of communication are, for some reason, not open.

One of the ways in which choreographers improve communication to audiences is by using repetition, reiteration, motif and development (see Chapter 2 above). Broadly we may say that encoders, whether artists, preachers or politicians, who build repetition into their messages are audience-centred, that is, they care about communicating their messages. Those who do not might be more concerned about subject matter or form (e.g. visual artists). So repetition, reiteration and development are primarily concerned with the efficiency of communication. Choreographers who engage in narrative (story-telling works, with plot and characters) communicate through movement choices, together with the way they depict relationships, costumes, sets and music choices.

In choreography that deliberately sets out to challenge audience perception, such as 'abstract' or 'non-literal' works, the lines of communication are deliberately not so clear. Consider, for example, how we might respond to unconventional behaviour in the street; we may not know how to 'read' that behaviour if it is unusual or seemingly outside normal conventions. Dancing in a shopping mall, stripping off on the football field, or shouting in a church are examples of behaviour that breaks conventions. We may also choose to study artists who have broken artistic conventions. A list of characteristics of early Impressionist paintings might include relatively small, thin, yet visible brush strokes, open composition, an emphasis on the accurate depiction of light in its changing qualities, the inclusion of *movement* as a crucial element of human perception and experience, and unusual visual angles. These elements challenged nineteenth-century understandings of representational painting. Similarly the first performances of the play *Waiting for Godot* (1948/9) by Samuel Beckett challenged audiences in the theatre. Beckett, an avant-garde writer who introduced new forms of writing for the novel and the play, introduced the Theatre of the Absurd. *Waiting for Godot* is an absurdist play where two characters, Estragon and Vladimir, wait for a character called Godot who never comes.

I hope that it has become evident to readers that Dance Studies as a discipline is clearly able to interact with theories and ideas from many other disciplines. My own view is that by embracing theoretical frameworks from performance studies, cultural studies, gender studies, anthropology, aesthetics and many others, we utilize fresh critical and analytical tools which enlighten our studies and help us to interrogate. Thus we borrow from other fields, but Dance Studies can also inform other disciplines and provide new discourse.

The second edition of *The Routledge Dance Studies Reader* (Carter and O'Shea, 2010) indicates very well how this new discourse works. Important articles from the first edition are accompanied by 22 new pieces of writing by dance academics world-wide. Stephanie Jordan and Helen Thomas (1998, 2010) introduce Roman Jakobson's ideas on linguistics and poetics in the chapter 'Formalism and Semiotics Reconsidered':

> Jakobson (1972) sets out six linguistic functions of communication which can be applied fruitfully to other modes of communication apart from verbal language: the referential, the emotive, the cognitive, the phatic, the metalinguistic and the poetic.... There are two major forms of semiotic expression, the referential (objective, cognitive) function, on the one hand, and, on the other, the emotive (subjective, expressive) function. These two functions are closely related and yet antithetical to each other. They combine what Jakobson (ibid) calls 'the double function of language'. Each function involves different modes of perception, one with understanding, the other with feeling and, as a result, they embrace two different modes of meaning.
>
> (Jordan and Thomas, 2010: 152)

Effectively, where the referential function dominates, the analysis will be with denotation or 'signing', and where the poetic function is dominant, the focus will be on connotation or symbolizing. In connotative analysis, where the poetic function is primary, the focus might be on intrinsic meaning or structure *within* the dance work. The referential function often refers to elements in the cultural context – *outside*, in the worlds shared by artist and spectator. To learn more about this extrinsic function, we turn our attention now to some of the many interrelationships to be drawn between dance and culture:

> Culture is 'a system of symbols thanks to which human beings confer a meaning on their own experience. Systems of symbols,

created by people, shared, conventional, ordered and obviously
learned, furnish them with an intelligible setting for orienting
themselves in relation to others or in relation to a living work
and to themselves'.

(Geertz, 1973: 130)

DANCE AND IDENTITY

In the latter half of the twentieth century, there was a steadily
growing interest in social or political function in dance, both in the
making of dances, and in methods of analysis. Despite the tendency
in modernism or post-modernism to reject or de-emphasize social
or political engagement, we cannot study dance and its meaning
without considering the many concerns and visibility of culture and
society, whether through identity, race, ethnicity, class or gender.

If we explore the relationship between dance/performance,
culture and politics, this also leads us to asking pertinent questions
about the sociology of knowledge. 'Every performance, if it is
intelligible as such, embeds features of previous performances:
gender conventions, racial histories, aesthetic traditions – political
and cultural pressures that are consciously and unconsciously
acknowledged' (Diamond, 1991).

Appreciating dance means that, as well as discussing differences and
distinctions between academic writings that deal specifically with
the aesthetics of the dance discipline, we should also familiarize ourselves with writing that involves issues of politics and culture. As
students of dance, you need to investigate and interrogate the ways
in which popular culture, mass media, art and everyday life have
political meaning and become sites for political action.

In mapping the territory of performance and culture, we
become aware of a number of definitions of the term 'political': e.g.
political theatre in terms of attacking the state or the monarchy; or
as propaganda (agitprop); or as alternative, feminist or community
theatre; or as debates or conflicts of subjectivity and identity
defined in terms of gender, race, class and sexuality – that is, the
highlighting of cultural difference.

For example, let us consider what kinds of relationship can be
identified between art, culture and politics, and the nature of those

interrelationships. Consider the intersection between cultural production and political action, such as the issues raised in Janet Wolff's *The Social Production of Art* (1981) – central ideas about the sociology of the arts which are still pertinent to us. The primary focus here is on the social nature of the arts in their production, distribution and reception, and a second but equally important issue is how art as a social product has to conceptualize the individual creativity of the artist, or author, or choreographer. In the twentieth century, there has been a growth of national sponsorship of the arts, rather than the traditional patronage systems whereby wealthy benefactors supported artists. But who makes the decisions about which artists or companies should be funded, and what kinds of criteria are used to make those decisions? What makes some artists successful and others fail to gain sponsorship? And in these systems, is it possible for a funding body to be neutral? Other issues in the arts relate to questions such as:

- What is worth knowing, and who makes the value judgement? How do those value judgements change in times of governmental change? Consider recent shifts in dance education in the last 20 to 30 years, and how those changes in strategy and approach have come about.
- What kinds of comparisons can be made between the notions of accessibility (for example, dance that everyone can understand and enjoy) and marginalization (dance which is considered more difficult, more elitist)? Which of these might be considered more important in your own country today, and why?
- In countries where censorship exists, what is considered acceptable as dance performance, and who makes the decisions about what should and should not be seen by audiences?

Let us take the example of Arthur Mitchell, who established the first African American classical ballet company Dance Theatre of Harlem in 1969. As the only African American dancer with the New York City Ballet from 1956 until 1970 – a factor which challenged the stereotypes of most major ballet companies at the time – he performed in all the major ballets in its repertoire, including *A Midsummer Night's Dream*, *The Nutcracker*, *Bugaku* and *Agon*. George Balanchine, choreographer and director of the NYCB, created the

pas de deux in *Agon* especially for Mitchell and although he danced
this role with white partners all over the world, it was never shown
on commercial television before 1965 as the Southern states refused
to carry it.

What kinds of political attitudes brought about such a situation?
Today it is sometimes easy to forget what kinds of struggles have
been faced by artists, women, ethnic minorities and the disadvan-
taged. A particularly well-developed arena of scholarship in the
dance discipline is that of gender, and particularly feminist writing:

> Gender systems are always political in the most fundamental
> sense of articulating a division of power. They operate in
> complex and often contradictory ways and intersect with other
> categories of social differentiation such as race, class, ethnicity,
> age, national origin, and so on.
>
> (Desmond, 1999: 309)

LOOKING AT GENDER

'Gender Studies' is an interdisciplinary study which analyses race,
ethnicity, sexuality and location. In Gender Studies, the term 'gender'
is used to refer to the social and cultural constructions of masculinities
and femininities, not to the state of being male or female. The philosopher Simone de Beauvoir said in her book *The Second Sex* (1949,
1989): 'One is not born a woman, one becomes one.'

Central to Gender Studies is an understanding of masculinity
and femininity as identity categories and relations of unequal
power. The University of Sussex (UK) website of the Centre for
Gender Studies asks:

> In 1790, a man in a wig was a prince of fashion; in 1970 a man
> in a toupee was a source of amusement: why? Why is it that
> more than thirty years after the passage of the Equal Pay Act,
> women working full time still earn 13% less than men do?
> Almost 50,000 women are raped each year in the UK; why is
> the conviction rate still at under 6 per cent?

Gender categorizes social difference, and provides methods and
frameworks for analysis of cultures, power, economies, the arts and

everyday experiences. Of particular interest to students of Dance and Performance Studies are the ways in which masculinity and femininity are constructed and represented. The study of gender, and particularly the discipline of feminism, introduces students to some conceptual and theoretical frameworks which facilitate understanding of the production and reception of powerful representations of masculinities, femininities and sexualities, and how gendered discourses operate in different spheres. Feminist theories can offer Dance Studies new readings of dance works, and can also influence the way we make and perform dance. We are influenced too by Film and Media Studies when addressing some of the ways in which gender is constructed and represented in art, literature and popular culture, and by representations in history and culture. Of particular interest in the current literature are key issues in feminism, masculinity and queer theories (see Burt, 1998, 2007; Midgelow, 2007; Claid, 2006; Fisher and Shay, 2009).

How can gender, in all its stereotypes and cultural practices, help us understand how dance is produced, interpreted and read? The ways that dance is codified arise from social customs, and these are often perpetuated both in training systems and in methods of dance-making. For example, in the classical tradition, females learn pointe work, and practise pirouettes and fouettés on the spot, whereas males have separate classes for elevation and the specific large and energetic jumps that circle the stage in so many of the traditional ballets. In pas de deux work, the normal tendency is for men to do the supporting and lifting of their partner; movement tends to be gendered. Indeed, ballet scenarios have often been chosen so that the protagonists, one male, one female, can engage in intense, loving relationships that conform to societal norms. In the 1960s and 1970s, three-act ballets with themes of romance, love, passion, regret and possible death were created by many of the major (male) choreographers: Antony Dowell and Antoinette Sibley in Frederick Ashton's *The Dream* (1964), Margot Fonteyn and Rudolf Nureyev in Kenneth MacMillan's *Romeo and Juliet* (1965), John Cranko's *Onegin* (1965) for Stuttgart Ballet and Ashton's *A Month in the Country* (1976) all presented images of acceptable social and artistic conventions. Young, beautiful, talented females live their lives through their love and dependency on the chosen man, however unacceptable he may be.

In modern dance too, love relationships both dramatic and lyrical were perpetuated in the works of Graham, Limón, Ailey and Taylor. But here the conventions change: as dance began exploring deeper emotional and psychological imperatives, the process of choreography became 'making visible the interior landscape' (Graham, 1950: 21–22). In many of Graham's works – *Cave of the Heart* (1946), *Errand into the Maze* (1947), *Clytemnestra* (1958) – the feminine body is forceful, dynamic and violently active. Indeed, in many of Graham's works, the male roles seem inconsequential in relation to the matriarchal roles she created for herself. Limón's *The Moor's Pavane* (1949) distils Shakespeare's tragedy *Othello* into a quartet of the four main characters, Othello, Desdemona, Iago and Emilia, with the strong passions of the dancers contained in the structure of a formal court dance.

In the post-modern era, there were many new challenges to gender, as discussed in Chapter 3 above. In Contact Improvisation, dance is created through collaborative interaction, usually in twos, and the gender of the dancers is often immaterial. They improvise together using touch, weight, momentum and gravity, and are involved in experiencing and sensing their own movement and that of their partner. It is important to develop a mutual trust, to be spontaneous, to go with the flow, and to keep an internal focus. Steve Paxton and the group of colleagues who first developed this form in 1972 were searching for a released form of movement. Banes (1987: 57) describes it as a 'democratic duet format incorporating elements of martial arts, social dancing, sports and child's play'. With its aspirations of equality and spontaneity, Contact Improvisation related to the then current attitudes of some aspects of American culture, but it soon spread to Europe and beyond as a method of generating dance content, an aesthetic performance form, a social or therapeutic tool, or a form of political statement.

When we ask, then, what kinds of femininity and masculinity are represented by dance, the answers are bound to be related to the period of history, the specific culture, the dance genre and the philosophic approach of dancer or choreographer.

As regards representations of gender, two interesting case studies drawn from the early twentieth century are Isadora Duncan and Vaslav Nijinsky. Isadora Duncan was a serious artist with specific goals, but in terms of sexual politics she is remembered more for her emancipation from the traditional roles of wife and mother, for an unconventional lifestyle and her desire for sexual freedom. The sensationalism which followed her during her lifetime tends to persist. Her artistic influence – advocating naturalness, drawing on ordinary movement of the body as dance content rather than any codified technique, simplicity and economy – has now been partially subsumed by the issues of modernism that were explored in the 1960s through the use of pedestrian movement, the revealing of dance's essential qualities, abstraction of forms and the desire to eliminate external references as subject (Banes, 1987: xv).

For many post-modern or independent dance artists, dance needed to be made more accessible. It needed to free the body from technique and theatricality, and explore time and space (see Chapter 3 above), and at the same time engage with cultural and societal issues.

To study dance history is also to study how the body carries social meaning. Burt (2010) describes how Nijinsky's virtuoso roles in works like *Le Spectre de la Rose* (1911) are aided by Fokine's choreography; jumps coincide with musical climaxes, and spatially there are circles that boldly encompass the stage, and strong diagonals to give the appearance of Nijinsky mastering the space. These are devices for displaying traditional male virtuosity. But Burt also goes on to explain that heterosexual male norms are generally maintained through keeping male sexuality invisible; any explicit expression of male sexuality was against conventions of nineteenth-century gender ideology, and yet many contemporary descriptions of Nijinsky ascribe androgynous qualities to his dancing, stressing its male power and strength but female sensuousness (Burt, 2010: 223).

In the 1980s, two avant-garde choreographers, Karole Armitage in the USA and Michael Clark in the UK, brought new challenges to the classical tradition: 'as exemplary postmodernists of the 1980s, they traffic in ... astonishment, one that wryly mixes classicism and kitsch, the high modern and the vulgar, abstraction with eroticism, the beautiful with the satanic – and the sardonic' (Banes, 1994: 297).

Sex and gender were at the heart of the works of both Clark and Armitage in the 1980s; both had trained in ballet and had become gifted performers and choreographers, reacting to what they perceived as antiquated codes that they experienced in training and particularly the rigidly accepted gender definitions of male and female.

In *The Watteau Duets* (1984), Armitage explored erotic and sadistic elements of the pas de deux, wearing spiked heels; her male partner wore a leather skirt. While she assaulted the senses of her audience with punk music, she claimed to be making ballets 'for this time', the present. In her hands, the classical dance vocabulary was given a shock to its system with speed and fractured lines, abstractions and asymmetry. Her choreography tends to follow in the Balanchine tradition of abstraction and pure movement, using classical ballet as a foundation upon which to create a new movement vocabulary. The principles that she uses to guide her when making dances include:

- seek beauty
- show mutability
- move like a blaze of consciousness
- perfection is the devil
- express the eroticism of gravity (www.armitagegonedance.org).

Michael Clark's early works also challenged dance audiences, as he tended to put on stage outrageous content, various sexual identities and cross-dressing in works like *New Puritans* (1984), *Our caca phoney H Our caca phoney H* (1985) and *I am Curious Orange* (1988). One of Clark's favourite bands, The Fall, was responsible for the music of this successful venture and introduced dance to a legion of new fans. His work was always fascinating, sometimes shocking, including bare bottoms and crude language, despite the fact that the dance itself was often neo-classical in style. Clark's more recent choreography contains provocative humour and an eclectic mixing of styles and genres, but his last three works seem to have abandoned much of his earlier angst; they are a trilogy of pieces to Stravinsky (www.michaelclarke.com).

Valerie Briginshaw (in Campbell, 1996) argues that both Armitage and Clark tend to celebrate commodification uncritically. Her article 'Postmodern Dance and the Politics of Resistance' analyses *Perfect Moment* (1992) by Lea Anderson as a post-modern text.

Though there is no single meaning, the work interrogates gender power systems and representation in a number of different ways. For example, Anderson presents the audience with images of women manipulating men, and men manipulating women. By dressing females and males identically in towelling bathrobes, and having them massage hands and feet, and various other body parts in unison, she reveals that typically masculine or feminine codes of behaviour and dress are culturally constructed. She uses a 'screen kiss' as a media sign of heterosexuality as a romantic ideal, and then subverts it by repeating the moment with three differently composed couples. At another moment, all performers regardless of gender wear shoulder-length feminine wigs and perform images parodying shampoo adverts: they 'turn and walk away from camera, swinging their hips in a consciously "camp" parody of female backing groups like The Supremes' (Briginshaw in Campbell, 1996: 128).

CONTINUATION . . .

Dance students enter university or college with a strong sense of discipline, developed from having been involved in dance training. They can also demonstrate the kinds of knowledge and understanding that allow them to matriculate (qualify) for entry to a university programme. Now, as students, they develop the ability to become critical thinkers, clear about the purpose at hand. They question information, interrogating points of view, and the conclusions of others. They develop and hone the skills that allow them to be clear, accurate, precise and relevant, whether doing research, preparing an essay, or presenting a lecture-demonstration. They apply logical reasoning and fairness to their reading, writing, observing, analysing and evaluation. They learn to conceptualize, to think, to apply different kinds of problem-solving, and to reason.

And then they proceed to the second year of their programme.

APPLIED DANCE STUDIES

In many countries of the world, dancing is the most popular physical activity after football. For example, in the UK, 4.8 million people dance in one way or another; one can find classes at all levels and styles in ballet, modern and contemporary forms, Asian and African styles, Irish or street dance, Morris or clog dancing, ballroom, Latin or freestyle dance, etc. Each of these has its own methods of training and educating the body to prepare it for performance. In addition, every weekend people go clubbing or to festivals or raves and engage in social dancing that needs no training, but rather is an expression of self, culture, courtship or group solidarity.

Some Dance programmes offer study units in these areas in order to explore and investigate the functions of dance in a particular society or culture. Historical Dance might introduce you to medieval dances that contain working actions like the washerwoman's branle, or to the pavanes and galliards of the courts of Henry VIII or Elizabeth I; in South Asian Dance Studies we might learn about specific dances of the various regions of India, Bangladesh or Pakistan, or their contemporary applications in European or North American cultures. We might also study the ways in which dance forms have travelled and taken hold in another culture from the one where it originally belonged, like flamenco or belly dancing.

For example, some vocational dance programmes in the Netherlands study urban dance forms developed from American influences, youth culture or immigrant populations, which had taken hold in Amsterdam, Rotterdam or Utrecht; in the USA, Australia and New Zealand, it is possible to study aspects of the culture of indigenous populations such as the American Indians, the

Aboriginal or Torres Strait Islanders, or Māoris. For example, Kapa haka, a traditional Māori performance art form, is still popular today and is well known worldwide from the sports fixtures of the New Zealand All Blacks rugby union team. It includes *haka* (posture dance), *poi* (dance accompanied by song and rhythmic movements of the *poi*, a light ball on a string), *waiata-ā-ringa* (action songs) and *waiata koroua* (traditional chants).

Dance anthropological studies, sometimes called dance ethnology or ethnography, means studying the dance in a culture, examining what dance means and how it operates; asking such questions as 'What are its traditions and its values?' We might investigate how notions of gender or status are constructed in particular dances, or how dance has become a method of organizing life experiences such as ritual or courtship. Scholars have examined the Polynesian-based dances of the Cook Islanders, the *lakalaka* (song-dance) of Tonga, or cultural dances from most countries in Africa or South America, and have investigated how dances feature as part of the social structure, as do the folk dances and music of Hungary. Both dancers and scholars have demonstrated great interest in this aspect of Dance Studies: American scholars such as Adrienne Kaeppler, Anya Peterson Royce, Joann Keali'inohomoku and Allegra Fuller Snyder have all contributed to the development of the discipline, as did two African American dancers, Pearl Primus and Katherine Dunham. Dunham's study of the dances of Haiti demonstrated how important dance can be to a society – as important as any other facet of social life. This is not the case in many Western countries, however, where the attitudes of the church prevailed, and dance was considered frivolous, transient and certainly less serious than the other art forms.

On every street corner of parts of New York and other cities in the United States today, however, urban dance forms such as hip hop abound, and a number of study texts have already been written. Forman and Neal edited a huge amount of material about hip hop and its culture in their *That's the Joint: The Hip Hop Studies Reader* (2004). Films like *The Freshest Kids: A History of the B-boy* (2002), *Style Wars* (1983) and *Rize* (2005) document the history of hip hop with many of the original founders like Kool Herc and The Rock Steady Crew. But the most extensive work on the history of hip hop is Jeff Chang's *Can't Stop Won't Stop* (2005). It chronicles the hip hop culture's rise from the ashes of the 1960s in the Bronx, New York, through cultural criticism and political analysis. *Can't Stop Won't Stop* is a detailed narrative based on interviews with DJ's, b-boys, rappers and members of the hip hop generation in the United States.

Much more has been written about socio-cultural aspects of dance, and many programmes of study will investigate these through specially written modules, probably in the second or third year. The next sections of this chapter identify ways in which dance has been established and applied in three other areas of our discipline, in educational, community and technology contexts, and discusses some of the ways in which you might be introduced to their histories and applications in your Dance Studies courses.

DANCE IN EDUCATION

Many young people come to Dance Studies in the tertiary sector from their experiences of creative dancing in junior school, O level or GCSE dance courses in secondary school, dance education in K–12 education (primary and secondary schooling) or equivalent. Many countries do not yet offer dance education in the public/state sectors, or at least not compulsorily. The first part of the section will therefore draw on some educational theories and influences that have affected education/training strategies where some form of dance in the primary and secondary sectors exists.

Dance in arts education in the USA found its first home in K–12 and higher education in physical education programmes. The first dance major was approved in the Women's Physical Education Department at the University of Wisconsin/Madison in 1926. Until the 1970s, most school and university dance programmes were affiliated with girl's/women's physical education. Legislation in 1972 and 1974 caused PE to focus on coeducational sports, and dance began to migrate into fine arts and performing arts departments. Over three decades, professional preparation and pedagogy in dance changed dramatically; dance educators were trained in creative and artistic processes (creating, performing and analysing dance). However, in K–12 education, best estimates indicate there may be 6,000 schools in the United States that offer dance as part of the K-12 curriculum, though only 7 per cent of those students are taught by qualified dance specialists. It is reported that approximately 57 per cent of American children receive no training in dance education (www.ndeo.org).

In some parts of Europe, the tendency has been to separate vocational dance training or amateur dance from university study, and educational dance for young people within the school system is rare. In the UK, however, we can trace some significant shifts in the history of the tradition:

Pre-Second World War: social dance and physical recreation
1945–1970: modern educational dance and expressive creativity
1970–1988: artistic discipline and formality
From 1989 – the National Curriculum and beyond.

Pre-Second World War: social dance and physical recreation

From 1900 until the Second World War, traditions of dance in British education emphasized social dance forms, folk forms, physical recreation and basic movement training. These were linked to the provision of popular education, the wider movement of health reform and the influence of radical thinkers and educational reformers such as Pestalozzi (1746–1827) and Froebel (1782–1852). Syllabi in physical education advocated dancing steps, musical drill, singing and marching, all highly formal and disciplined, contrasted with freer movement, which was considered more natural. A growing consciousness of national heritage brought a revival of English folk dances and, in addition, three forms of modern dance originated in Britain. These were natural movement (Madge Atkinson), the revived Greek dance (Ruby Ginner) and Margaret Morris movement. The Swiss Emile Jaques-Dalcroze's eurhythmics (a system of training musical sensibility through the translation of rhythm into bodily movements) was also influential.

Two contrasting impulses were evident: the highly choreographed and spatially exact social and folk dances, which need to be taught didactically and in groups, and the beginnings of creative and dynamic dance expression in the curriculum, which require a different and freer approach and engage children as individuals. The differences between the first impulse – the importance of the dance – from the second – the importance of the responses of the child/student – can be seen to have a significant effect on the relationship of the teacher and those who are learning, whether pupils or students. That is, the teaching style must change if individualistic responses are to be encouraged. The influences of these ideas continued and developed in the UK throughout the 1930s and 1940s, and changes in the social/cultural context after the Second World War together with the 1944 Education Act provided a new context of receptivity for the modern educational dance based on the principles of Rudolf Laban.

Modern educational dance and expressive creativity: 1945–1970

Rudolf Laban was 'recognised as a major theorist of movement and as an innovator of modern dance' (Wilson, 1997: 5). The application of his work to educational dance in schools in the UK is well documented by practitioners such as Redfern, Preston-Dunlop and Smith-Autard. Extraordinarily, the movement principles developed by a particular individual for applications in theatre and communities in Germany became predominant in educational terms in the UK.

When Rudolf Laban arrived in the UK as a refugee in 1938, he left behind a distinctive career in Europe as performer, choreographer, director, educationalist and mentor. He had already applied his philosophic ideas and systematic analysis of human movement to a variety of contexts in dance, acting and performance, and in notation, psychotherapy, non-verbal communication and ergonomics (Hodgson and Preston-Dunlop, 1992; Preston-Dunlop, 1998; McCaw. 2011). Though Laban's ideas were new to the majority in the UK, they had developed from as early as 1912 in Switzerland and Germany, and his pupils had gradually established Laban schools and dance companies in some of the main German cities.

Laban's influence on the physical education curricula in England from the 1940s was quite profound. The inclusion of modern educational dance or 'movement' within the curriculum of many schools in the 1940s and 1950s suggests a working knowledge of Laban's concepts and agreement with his view that dance offered children opportunities for 'creativity, imagination and individuality' (Smith-Autard, 1994: 9). The move towards more progressive education in the UK encapsulated in the 1944 Education Act coexisted with Laban's ideas.

General education in the 1950s UK adopted teaching and learning strategies that were increasingly child-centred and process-oriented, and these developed and extended into the 1960s. It is clear that the interpretation and practical application of Laban's theories were well used by physical education teachers. Laban believed in the dancer as creator as well as interpreter. He emphasized the mastery of movement and personal expression and the importance of dance play, improvisation and experimentation. He promoted synthesis between understanding dance and practising dance, and these notions were adapted for use with young people in practical dance education sessions in school.

Laban and his colleague Lisa Ullmann used approaches to the making of dance that concentrated on exploration, discovery and problem-solving to find movement language relating to body action, dynamics and use of the dance space. Using these methods, a teacher can act as initiator, guide, facilitator or collaborator, or indeed choose to utilize more didactic or instructive methods when necessary to provide a range of creative dance-composing situations that engage students both practically and cognitively.

The educational climate of the immediate post-war period in Europe was generally conducive to change under the influence of the American John Dewey's educational theory, which emphasized the child's natural curiosity as a motivating factor towards self-discovery of knowledge (Dewey, 1934, 1958). Teachers, it was felt, should design and facilitate problem-solving activities so that the child's innate curiosity could be developed and refined through practical experiences, by learning through doing.

In his publication of *Modern Educational Dance* in 1948, Laban introduced a systematic application of these basic theories for use in schools. The ideas in this text were subsequently developed and further exemplified by Valerie Preston in *A Handbook for Modern Educational Dance* (1963), and during the 1950s and 1960s modern educational dance became the form of dance usually taught in teacher training colleges and schools. The rationale made for this form of dance in schools was driven by the concepts of a child's natural physicality, the need for kinaesthetic awareness, personality development and social interaction (Adshead, 1981: 25–26; Redfern, 1973; North, 1971). These concepts provided the fundamental general principles for the processes of dance-making in both education and community contexts.

In the Introduction to *Modern Educational Dance* Laban wrote:

> In schools where art education is fostered, it is not artistic perfection or the creation and performance of sensational dances which is aimed at, but the beneficial effect of the creative activity of dancing upon the personality of the pupil.
>
> (1948: 11–12)

Laban's text also emphasized the importance of children understanding intellectually what is being experienced practically: 'the new dance technique endeavours to integrate intellectual knowledge with creative ability, an aim which is of paramount importance in any form of education' (Laban 1948: 13).

Ideas that had been developing through the varied aspects of his career in Germany – as a teacher, choreographer, director, researcher, in the theatre, in the private sector of education and in therapy – were now thoughtfully applied to the British post-war education situation. Laban's philosophy and concepts offered a new approach to physical training, a clear set of principles and a holistic view of the child as an individual, and these were clearly taken up by teachers and advisers both regionally and nationally.

At the time, the potential of Laban's work in other spheres was almost totally ignored. The experience of running his dance company Tanzbühne Laban, of establishing a Choreographisches Institut in 1926 and his appointment as choreographer at the Opera House in Berlin from 1929 demonstrate that he possessed considerable skills and knowledge of professional choreography. Yet the opportunity to apply these skills in Britain in the 1940s and 1950s never materialized, except through the work of Kurt Jooss and Sigurd Leeder. The professional dance genre of the period remained predominantly based in the classical ballet traditions and relationships (see Chapter 3 above).

Yet Laban's ideas have influenced pedagogic thinking in many countries of the world, supporting the notion that shared problem-solving and decision-making engaged in during the creation of a group dance can be of real value educationally. That is, it can be of value as part of the *artistic* process or as an aspect of the *social* process. Whichever objective is intended there is no doubt that the experience of dance through working together in small group inter-actions is quite distinct from learning a dance developed by a chore-ographer or taught by a teacher as a series of steps and patterns, though of course all these experiences offer different kinds of value.

It is evident that Laban's ideas offer valuable opportunities to Dance Studies students from several points of view. See, for example, Bill Evans's chapter 'Teaching Movement Analysis' in Chazin-Bennahum (2005). As Professor of Dance at the University of New Mexico from 1988 to 2004, Evans describes how all undergraduate majors and minors studied Laban/Bartenieff Move-ment Analysis for two semesters, first to facilitate a process of self-discovery, and then to acquire theoretical tools to be used in creative problem-solving. Laban's classification of movement com-prises four major components, which are usually termed body, effort, space and relationship (Preston, 1963). The emphasis is on training as a holistic approach, framed by a set of movement prin-ciples rather than by codified techniques. Through the use of this theoretical framework for movement, which can be used in both creative and analytical situations, we can generate new movement for dance and examine it once it is formed.

Body: The emphasis is on our kinaesthetic sense and on the mastery of the body as an instrument of expression. That means analysis of the action and motion of the body, including such aspects as posture, gesture, weight transference, travelling, stillness, elevation and turning.

Effort: The emphasis is on studying dynamics or qualities of move-ment, the components of which are time, weight, space and flow. Effort involves an analysis of how the body moves in terms of:

- time – from suddenness to sustainment;
- weight – from firm to fine touch, or strong and light;
- space in the body – from direct to flexible action;
- the flow of energy, from free flow to bound flow; and
- all the possible combinations of these elements.

Space: The emphasis is on studying spatial orientation, or where the body moves in space, including levels, directions, extension, stable (dimensional) and labile (diagonal) movement.

Relationship: The emphasis is on the changing relationship of body parts, of dancers or to the location, set or work/performance space.

Thus from the points of view of the development of the young dance artist *and* dance educator, Laban Movement Analysis offers a useful tool for formal dance analysis, but can be equally valuable in exploring and learning to manipulate the materials of choreography, that is, in exploration and creation.

Laban's movement principles (kinaesthetic awareness of the body, dynamic and spatial awareness and relationship), together with notions of spontaneity (the ability to play, explore movement, be creative in improvisatory terms), of the fostering of artistic expression, the ability to observe and to understand intellectually what is being experienced practically, are all important aspects of dance education for young people.

Educational theories

Early studies of teaching identify notions of teachers' styles rather simplistically, as either authoritarian or democratic, and this was a key concern during the mid-twentieth century. The origin of this polarity lies in the approach to the structure and organization of knowledge. A brief examination of two opposing educational ideologies, the classical and romantic views of knowledge and curriculum, demonstrates this. The classical view sees the curriculum as the induction of young members of society into established forms of thought and understanding, whereas the romantic view considers education as an integral part of life rather than of the adult world, and stresses experience, awareness and creativity (Lawton, 1973: 22). A summary of these two positions is set out in Table 6.1.

In dance education we can see that the classical view tends to be advocated in the conservatoire, academy or vocational/professional schools where traditionally the major objective is the acquisition of an extremely high level of practical performance skill, whether in

Table 6.1 Two opposing educational ideologies

Classical	Romantic
Subject-centred	Child-centred
Skills	Creativity
Instruction	Experience
Information	Discovery
Obedience	Awareness
Conformity	Originality
Discipline	Freedom

violin playing, painting or classical ballet. The development of these skills is reliant on the practical transmission of expertise and competence dominated by a disciplined, didactic approach to instruction. By contrast, characteristics of the romantic view can be recognized in the maintained, state-sector dance education of the 1950s and 1960s, as described earlier, with an emphasis on learning as process, and learners being active in applying their knowledge. This 'instruction versus discovery' debate is seen in Table 6.2

Table 6.2 Chart demonstrating theories of R.F. Dearden (1965)

Instruction	Discovery
Known as the elementary school tradition	Known as the developmental tradition
Relative to the teacher	Relative to the learner
Teacher as instructor	Teacher as facilitator

Teaching seen as 'directly imparting knowledge' through
    Rote learning, drilling, repetition
    Formal instruction
    Skills acquisition
	Learning seen as 'finding out', teacher guides experience through
	    Exploring, and encountering failure as well as success
	    Abstractionism, or making explicit what has been learned
	    Problem-solving

Learning by experience: teacher using such devices as questioning, hinting, commenting, professing ignorance	Learning by experience individually, with peers

Artistic discipline and formality: 1970–1988

In the UK, the climate of expressive creativity in education had changed significantly by the 1970s. The emphasis shifted to one that increasingly stressed the performed product and a developing aspiration towards technical skill and developing knowledge of theatre dance performance. Technical training systems from American modern dance or classical ballet were introduced to complement or replace modern educational dance forms, and attention turned to the need for formal, objective assessment in the dance curriculum. This move was reflective of a shift in the arts generally (Bloomfield, 1989: 19).

An emphasis on technical skills development and contextual studies, including the history of theatre dance, developed, and tended to draw upon available exemplars from America where more university level courses existed, rather than from Europe. Texts were available, published in English, new techniques were being taught, particularly in London, and the works of contemporary dance choreographers from the USA and from Europe were available to view in performances by professional dance companies. The styles of dance most commonly taught in these courses are derived from the American tradition of modern dance (Graham or Cunningham; see Chapters 2 and 3 above). Examinations in dance choreography were established both in secondary/high school education and in Dance degree programmes, requiring the student to create dances and perform them.

By the early 1980s there was an increasingly rigorous focus on the arts in education in many countries in Europe. In the USA, dance programmes had tended to integrate artistic, educational and cultural values, and dance joined forces with music, visual arts and theatre to support national initiatives in arts education. However, in the UK there was a schism between the education and performance arenas, a crucial divide between professional dancers and choreographers in classical and contemporary dance companies, and the majority of dance educators. In 1982 Peter Brinson proposed that a successful collaboration between dancers and educators 'depends upon each being masters of their work and respecting the mastery of the others ... it requires sympathy, sensitivity, humility and mutual respect' (Brinson, 1982: 4). After consultation, the Arts

Council of Great Britain issued a firm policy statement advocating that its clients (those who received arts funding) should perceive their role and function in terms of educational involvement. The Council intended to adopt

> as one of the prime criteria of assessing clients' work, the extent and quality of efforts made to broaden the social composition of audiences, to develop response and to increase involvement in the arts. Each revenue client will be asked to provide a report of its work in this area when making an annual application.
>
> (Arts Council, 1983: 5)

This provided considerable growth in commitment and activity to dance-in-education within the major dance companies, not all of it successful, but at least creating some collaboration and greater understanding between artists and teachers. At best it provided an inspiring variety of projects and programmes that deeply engaged young people in the discipline of dance while pressing dance companies to consider more flexible and inventive approaches.

The National Curriculum and beyond

In 1989 the British education system introduced the National Curriculum which initiated more prescriptive, formulaic methods of teaching and making dance, setting definitive programmes of study and specific attainment targets and thus ignoring the individualized, specialist capabilities of established teachers. In order to establish concepts of good practice in dance education, and to aid expertise in its teaching, many universities and colleges found ways of synthesizing instructional teaching and learning through discovery. The curriculum tried to combine and integrate the whole of dance as an art, by identifying three interlocking strands as being of equal importance: dance performance, composition or choreography, and dance appreciation based on the theoretical framework developed by Smith-Autard in *The Art of Dance in Education*, which attempts a synthesis of elements of the 'educational' and 'professional' models into a new 'Midway' model (Smith-Autard, 1994: 26). This model is now utilized in the USA, Canada, Australia and New Zealand as well as parts of Europe. Meanwhile, Australia is just about to embark upon a National Curriculum; the Ausdance website (www. ausdance.org.au) has developed a new training programme to help dance teachers establish a skill set for teaching dance, in preparation for the start of dance in the Australian curriculum in 2012.

This history demonstrates clearly the extent to which dance education in schools has shifted in the last 40 years. The education (secondary and tertiary) sector in many countries now attempts to span a full range of choreographic processes and experiences, from directed, instructional teaching to open discovery and collaborative work. This means that those who enter Dance programmes at higher education level will have opportunities to develop a balance of skills which offers flexibility for future careers.

DANCE IN THE COMMUNITY

Everyone has the right freely to participate in the cultural life of the community, to enjoy the arts and to share in scientific advancement and its benefits.

(Article 27, The Universal Declaration of Human Rights)

The cultural needs of any post-modern society may be met by opportunities that stimulate and release the creativity of ordinary people, through emphasizing accessibility and participation. Matarasso (1994) outlines a coherent and workable theoretical underpinning for community-based arts work, defining art as a means through which:

we can examine our experience of ourselves, the world around us and the relationship between the two, and share the results with other people in a form which gives free rein to our intellectual, physical, emotional and spiritual qualities. This definition characterises art by purpose rather than type, the distinguishing system favoured by the arts establishment ... it places art's function of communication at the heart of its nature, so that any human activity which seeks to express individual or collective experience creatively may be termed art.

(Matarasso 1994: 4)

This sense of purpose can be identified in countries where there have been important developments in 'community dance' and 'amateur dance' in the past 30 years. Though these two terms 'community' and 'amateur' are often seen as problematic, in general we refer to non-professional dance activity outside formal educational spheres, where the focus is on the value of social interaction and the personal interests of individuals in relation to the creation of dance. But as Thomson (1988: 89) describes, the community dance movement 'might be characterised as an amateur movement led by professionals (and aspiring, when appropriate, to professional standards)', having the potential to bring dance back into the mainstream of our respective cultures. This might mean publicly funded dance projects, led by individual dance workers or small dance companies, which aim to 'stimulate, develop and co-ordinate dance activities within their community' (Rubidge in Thomson, 1988). Or equally, we might refer to social forms of dance (like country dancing or ceilidhs) which continue to be maintained and developed by members of the social community. We are not only speaking here about professional dancers, but about artist-practitioners or amateur leaders who demonstrate the ability to teach, choreograph, workshop, facilitate, devise, organize, manage and coach. The general term now used is 'community dance practitioners': this includes the whole spectrum of roles that relate to dance and the community. So, how did dance in the community come about, and how did it develop? As community arts tended to develop in the UK, Australia and Canada, my examples come from those countries. This section identifies some of the history of the ideas, and discusses how it might be studied and practised in a Dance Studies course.

Community arts developments in the mid-1980s

It is generally accepted that arts in the community may already exist in some form (for example, long-sword or rapper traditional dance in the north of England) or develop as a particular response to the cultural needs of a society, either initiated by individuals or by groups. Community arts in the UK emerged from the political and social thinking of the radical 1960s, and put forward a primary aim to provide opportunities that might stimulate and release the creativity of ordinary people, emphasizing accessibility, participation and relevance (Brinson, 1991; Kelly, 1984; Kershaw, 1992; Thomson, 1988: 88–98).

In 1968 in the UK, the Community Development Foundation (CDF) was set up to pioneer new forms of community development. A government-sponsored organization, the CDF aimed to strengthen communities by ensuring the effective participation of people in determining the conditions which affect their lives through influencing policy-makers, promoting best practice and providing support for community initiatives (Clinton, 1993: iii). Six years later a policy paper of the community arts advisory board of the Greater London Arts Association called for the use of art to 'effect social change and affect social policies' through the involvement of people on a collective basis. In addition it advocated the use of art forms 'to enjoy and develop people's particular cultural heritages ... community arts activists operate in areas of deprivation, using the term "deprivation" to include financial, cultural, environmental or educational deprivation' (Brinson, 1991: 123).

For some, the emphasis was on the political and cultural framework rather than specific arts practice; this later became known as the 'cultural democracy' argument. A contrasting position was offered by Sir Roy Shaw, who argued for the democratization of culture, claiming that this is to do with making the 'high arts' more accessible to working people (Kershaw, 1992: 184). Thomson notes that the word 'community' was used to counter the isolation of individuals which may have been the consequence of urban industrialization. He identifies three meanings of the term pertinent to the arts and to dance; 'community' as a geographical locality, as a local social system, or as a sense of identity (Thomson 1988: 92). A more interventionist approach is demonstrated by Owen Kelly, who stressed 'a set of shared social meanings ... constantly created and mutated through the actions and interactions of its members, and through their interaction with wider society' (Kelly, 1984: 100). These notions of interaction, intervention and social change are important aspects of the value of dance in community contexts.

In the UK, the community dance movement seemed to be influenced by three factors: the growth of the community arts movement, the adoption of American modern and post-modern dance methods, and the Laban-based educational dance in the education sector (Jasper, 1985: 181). The first three appointments of dance animateurs (that is, dance teachers who 'animated' or 'initiated' dance groups outside schools) – Molly Kenny, in Cardiff, Veronica Lewis in Cheshire, and Marie McClusky in Swindon – were made in 1977. These three innovators initiated the movement and by the early 1980s, community dance initiatives were being funded and guided by the objectives of local authority (local government) youth services, community and leisure services and social services. Contracts were often arranged in partnership with the regional arts boards, and a much broader range of activities then emerged.

Dance animateurs, who today are more often called community dance practitioners, work within a broad constituency of people. They facilitate and teach in classes and workshops, and through formal and informal performances, with youth groups, the elderly, people with all forms of special need, disability or disenfranchisement, including the unemployed, those in prisons or institutions, and people in hospital. The diversity of community-related activity makes it difficult to generalize, but all dance workers strive to make dance accessible and relevant to members of their community, involving themselves with teaching and administration, and acting as advocates for dance, introducing people to an art form which may be unfamiliar to them.

Particular skills are obviously needed for these roles: in a community context, the needs of the client group should be paramount. For example, if you are working with a group of people with learning difficulties, it would be foolish to impose certain kinds of traditional performance outcomes; it is more sensible to address concerns relating to the reality of where you are, why you are there and who are the members of your group. Thus, the work of the community dance practitioner is dependent upon the context and the brief of the job, the needs of the community and the interests of the individual. Often the traditional concepts of form, content and technical skill usually evident in professional dance performance need to be adapted or reconsidered, especially in the early stages of working together with a group. Performance outcomes are often secondary, or indeed immaterial, to the development of confidence, self-esteem and the ability to share that dance can offer. In working with a group of people with learning difficulties, an initial approach in the dance class might include some general movement sequences in a circle led by the group leader, then relationship play with partners or small groups, leading and following, or working with rhythmic or spatial patterns. That is, the needs of the individuals within the social group are essentially more important than the creation of a dance.

The notion of shared endeavour is a predominant mechanism for this work, as is the use of facilitating skills which involve open rather than closed strategies and joint decision-making. The usual distinctions between performer and audience, creation and participation, and production and consumption tend to disappear in this work. The creative processes are often valued by all participants more highly than the end product, and it is generally understood that any performance outcomes may not be formal (e.g. a theatre performance) or may not be appropriate at all.

For the Dance student, these experiences can be difficult to understand, but they often provide a watershed of understanding, a relinquishing of self-consciousness, and recognition of the power of dance as a shared experience and an instrument of social change. It is in the experiential that the function of community dance becomes validated. Rachel Liggitt, a student in her third year, wrote in 1991:

> Craig, an adolescent with Down's Syndrome, picked up a hoop that was in the centre of the circle as if it was the most precious object in the world; he lifts it high above his head and moves it gently and controlled through the space to his side. We all clapped in appreciation. Communication verbally within the dance session is of little importance. My aim is in allowing them to be themselves by setting up the right environment....
>
> To articulate in words the 'feeling experience' is a difficult task. I can describe the format of the sessions and can describe the physical movements of the body, but the essences of the series of sessions to date have involved a 'spiritual' experience, an experience which has been immensely powerful. As a facilitator, I have been drawn to the understanding that the essence of the work is to 'hold the space' ... my role is to provide a comfortable setting where we all have mutual appreciation and respect for one another. The 'power' of the circle is immense, it is a safe haven which is the arena by which we can share, show and perform.
>
> (Liggitt, 1991: 8)

In common with many graduates of Dance courses, this student went on to create a freelance career covering teaching, initiating workshops, the creation of community choreography and professional performance. The facilitation skills introduced in a dance and the community course and developed in performance and choreographic work, and the understandings that accrue from these experiences, are understood to be part of the 'toolbox' of the dance-devising processes. Rather than by applying conventional models and theories in the choreographic process, qualities such as awareness, sensitivity, the ability to reflect 'in the moment', and to respond appropriately to situations of uncertainty are considered apposite. This means developing *awareness* both of the context and of the individual members of the client group; *sensitivity* in terms of what is spoken and what is initiated in practical sessions, and how relationships are built and developed. The *ability to reflect* relates to Schön's concept of 'reflection-in-action', or 'thinking what they are doing whilst they are doing it' that practitioners bring to situations of uncertainty, uniqueness and conflict (Schön, 1987: 6).

Influences from community arts

In the community arts, the range of working practices go far beyond direct teaching; that is, we use terms like guiding, facilitating, 'workshopping', advising, mentoring, consulting, etc. The term 'facilitation skills' embraces these notions of awareness, sensitivity, reflection and being able to act 'in the moment', or reflection-in-action. According to Schön, when a practitioner makes sense of a situation he perceives to be unique, he is able to experiment on the spot, from a selective series of variations, in relation to the needs of the client, or the client group. The facilitator needs to have a clear sense of direction without really knowing in advance what the product will be. That is because in the devising process, facilitation implies that all members of the participating group have the opportunity to contribute to discovery and decision-making, and thus the end product is not one person's vision.

In dance and choreography contexts, the facilitator needs general knowledge and understanding of choreographic strategies, concepts and devices, and some experience of their application. This general knowledge is gained through practice and theory, in the studio and in the lecture room, from personal, peer and tutor experience and observation, and from gaining knowledge of publicly referenced works through videos, books, articles and websites. In a problem-solving situation, these become part of our repertoire, which means we are less likely to use formulaic methods.

A three-year integrated choreography programme, such as those introduced in many Dance Studies courses, offers the dance student the experience of learning a set of principles, which may be applied, modified and adapted as required by the career context. It is necessary that the programme you choose is flexible enough to ensure that, as dance students, you engage with the central con-cepts, methods and modes of enquiry within the discipline, and develop attributes such as individuality and autonomy, intelligence, empathy, empowerment, judgement and the capability for reflection.

Examples of community dance practice

The Foundation for Community Dance (www.communitydance. org.uk) is the professional organization in the UK for anyone involved in creating opportunities for people to experience and participate in dance. Its website says: 'Our vision is for a world where dance is a part of everyone's life, our mission to make par-ticipation in dance important to individuals, communities and society.'

In the words of Dr Peter Brinson, Ausdance, Australia's profes-sional dance advocacy organization (www.ausdance.org.au),

> embraces all aspects of dance from performance to teaching; from multicultural, social and recreational dance to the advance-ment of dancers' health. Above all, Ausdance focuses the cause and value of dance as a matter of concern for state and federal governments ... an organisation truly and visibly representative of the whole dance profession.

DANZ – Dance Aotearoa New Zealand (www.danz.org.nz) – is the national organization for New Zealand dance, and again it communicates a holistic approach to a wide range of dance activities, from classes and performances to workshop programmes, choreographic fellowships and a new NZ Disability and Dance Strategy.

In many other countries too, there is a similar desire to embrace and maintain dance participation as a part of the fabric of society, through many different organizations; in Canada, for example, there exist many forms of traditional dance, as Marion Rose explains:

> Anyone who has ever lived on the Canadian prairies knows what I'm talking about. At every wedding you will experience a repertoire of dances that reflects the ethnic origins of the original settlers: Czech, Polish, German, Scandinavian, Ukrainian. These include the Polka, Waltz, Two-step, Foxtrot, Schottische, Heel-toe polka, French Minuet, Seven Step, and everyone's favourite, the Butterfly. In some places you can add Square Dances, the Hop Polka, Virginia Reel, Kolomeike, and the Czech polka.
>
> (www.Marianrose.com)

The Aboriginal peoples of Canada include the Indian, Inuit and Métis peoples who practise both social and ceremonial music and dance events, such as the pow-wow, a gathering of North America's Native people. The word derives from the Narragansett word *powwaw*, meaning 'spiritual leader'. A modern pow-wow is a specific type of event where both Native American and non-Native American and Canadian people meet to dance, sing, socialize, and honour Native culture. There is generally a dancing competition, often with significant prize money awarded. Pow-wows vary in length from a one day session of five to six hours to three days. Pow-wows called for a special occasion can be up to one week long.

As we see, in many countries of the world, dance activities are organized for and by diverse social, amateur and community dance groups: from youth dance groups to mother and toddler sessions, from pow-wows to ceilidhs, large and small, formal and informal. Sometimes they spring out of the traditions of the people, and at other times they are started deliberately by organizations that wish to provide cultural activities for the public.

The reader can look up hundreds of these activities and projects on the World Wide Web.

As an example, I have chosen to mention dance activities which focus especially on older people. Old age has been described as the time between retirement and death, the rather role-less existence of 'the pensioner', and people in this age group often feel that they are not appreciated by society despite their intellectual abilities and wealth of experience. But as populations live longer and are often quite fit and healthy, dance has become a means of socializing, meeting friends, keeping fit and engaging in the arts all at the same time.

Dance events for senior citizens

In the dance world, professional dancers often start thinking about retiring at the age of 35, so it is unusual to see older dancers on stage, although everyone remembers that Margot Fonteyn first danced with Rudolf Nureyev when she was 42 and he 24, and that she retired from dancing at 60. An interesting recent phenomenon has been the development of dance groups and projects designed especially for the older population; here we look at two projects from Sweden and the UK where the emphasis is on choreographic work for the stage.

Efva Lilia, a choreographer and academic whose work has had a tremendous influence in Sweden (see www.efvalilia.se), researched the Movement as the Memory of the Body project between 2003 and 2006. She and her research group aimed to develop the expressive language of the stage to encompass older people as both participants and audience. One group was made up of four ex-professional dancers and two musicians aged between 65 and 84, and the second group consisted of 17 amateurs between 59 and 88. In the three years of the project they all spent hours in workshops and rehearsals, performed three choreographed works in 54 performances in Sweden, Norway, Iceland, Russia and Portugal, wrote diaries of their participation and received accolades from press and audience members.

The Company of Elders is an over-60s performance group based at Sadler's Wells in London. The Sadler's Wells website (www. sadlerswells.com) says:

Sadler's Wells' Creative Learning department, Connect, has long expressed the simple ethos of Lilian Baylis, one of the most visionary directors of Sadler's Wells, to make the arts accessible to everyone. In our contemporary lives, we recognise that dance connects people, promotes confidence and physical wellbeing. Our work prioritises community involvement, educational insight and challenges perceptions of who can dance.

Activities are carefully designed to suit all tastes and experiences, drawing on the diversity of Sadler's Wells dance programme. Our activities truly cater for all ages with local primary school children rubbing shoulders with our resident over 60s performers, Company of Elders.

The group has 30 members aged from 62 to 85, rehearses weekly, performs choreography created by professional choreographers, and has toured to international festivals and featured in a television programme *Imagine*, introduced by Alan Yentob for the BBC in 2009. There is now a long waiting list, as individuals realize the potential for creative activity and the fulfilment and energy generated by belonging to such a group. Video clips are available on www.sadlerswellsisdance.com/#/category/takingpart.

These video clips, and others like them on YouTube (www.youtube.com), introduce the last section in this chapter, which discusses the development of new study units in Dance Studies programmes based on the relationship of dance with technology. Here we investigate some of the aspects that might be covered in such modules as dance for camera; image, movement, performance; choreography for screen; or dance and visual media.

DANCE AND TECHNOLOGY

The domain of dance and technology usually starts with beginner study units which explore relationships between the body, choreography and technology through:

- study of basic techniques for shooting and editing material;
- live and recorded dance works, their histories and development;

- explorations with fixed and moving cameras, designing space, and shifts of perspective; or
- exploration of the moving body, and projections in performance.

As these courses continue through the second and third years of study, students can make choices as to how they might use technology to prepare dance resources, to record, edit and recreate their own dances, to upload their own choreographies to YouTube or other web-based resources, or create installations in galleries or museums. It seems that anything is possible, added to which there are new potential developments emerging every day.

Technology in performance can bring a number of new and different approaches, from the use of intelligent lighting and projections, to musical technology, live and mediated dances, real time, liveness, interactivity, embodiment and transformation, as discussed in the work of Auslander (1999), Birringer (1998, 2000), Chapple and Kattenbelt (2006) or Broadhurst and Machon (2007). Technology can evidently create a different awareness of self in relation to others (body parts dancing?) or become another element of a performance (digital projections?), and it can also take the place of the live performer altogether in favour of the mediated or virtual body (dancing with no live bodies?). Digital practices provide choreography with potential for numerous creative and aesthetic possibilities. A brief history might explain how these elements came about.

Terms such as videodance, dance-film, choreography for the camera, cinedance, and dance for the camera are used to describe various approaches to dance-based work dealing with the camera. Preston (2006: 76) says that 'Emphasis of the work is on dance or choreography, what that says about the hybrid field of dance and film/video and what it means for the reception and understanding of dance in general.' Dance-film and videodance tend to be engaged with non-commercial dance work that is specifically made for film/video. Screen-dance is used more broadly for camera-related dance, particularly commercial dance and screen adaptations of theatre-based work.

Traditionally, recording live dance in the theatre usually included showing all the steps, all the dancers, and all the entrances and exits. Companies often use these recordings to reconstruct the dance when it comes back into the repertoire with a new cast. Video-dance, on the other hand, has no rules, apart from the maker's intention and taste/aesthetic. We can make inanimate objects 'dance' just by using editing; we can juxtapose body parts in a random way, or make a dancer 'look' as though she is dancing on top of the Eiffel Tower or in the palm of someone's hand.

Some of the most popular dance on film was seen in the early movies of Busby Berkeley, Fred Astaire and Gene Kelly. Parallel with the work of Maya Deren who started avant-garde dancefilm, many developments with these dance film practitioners took place in Hollywood in the 1930s and 1940s and had different ways of dealing with film and dance. Berkeley was an innovative filmmaker but was more interested in aerial shots and the visual experience than in physical expression (Delamater, 1981). Fred Astaire incorporated the dance into the narrative, usually used full body shots and tried to get continuity by limiting the number of 'cuts'. Films like *Flying Down to Rio* (1933), *The Gay Divorcee* (1934) and *Top Hat* (1935) were very popular, and McRobbie (1990) called them 'classic narrative movies', which 'use dance as a metaphor for social identity, romantic fulfilment and other fantasies of achievement'. These ideas led later to the dance–film era of *Saturday Night Fever* (1977), *Fame* (1980), *Flashdance* (1983), *Staying Alive* (1983) and *Footloose* (1984).

Videodance in the 1980s was influenced by music videos (MTV culture) and advertisements, which had in common eye-catching images of the body, with 'the video–specific possibilities of electronic image modification, fast cutting and effects' (Rosiny, 1994). In the 1990s, many television channels started to commission 'shorts' – i.e. five-minute choreographies made especially for the screen, which had to be both inventive and interesting, and created a new genre and another place to dance. In these videodances the viewer is given a selected perspective since the camera leads the eyes to what they see, unlike seeing performances on the stage where each member of the audience can choose what to look at. Bob Lockyer, a television executive producer, was trying to relate to the 'normal' non-dance public, and these short videos were partly designed to bring dance into the living room.

Thierry de Mey, a Belgian musician and filmmaker, brought several adaptations of choreography to film from the dance companies of Wim Wanderkeybus (*Musique de tables*, 1998) and Anne Teresa de Keersmaeker (*Fase*, 2002; *Rosas danst Rosas*, 1996). His installations, in which music, dance, video and interactive processes work together, have been presented at events such as the Venice and Lyon biennials as well as in many museums. He recently worked with the choreographer William Forsythe to produce *One Flat Thing* (2008), which used sophisticated cinematic tools.

According to Sherrill Dodds (2004), features of videodance which are clearly not possible on stage include close-ups of the fragmented body, unusual locations and environments, the ability to play with spatial logic or to look from different perspectives as in a top shot, and the ability to reverse or repeat movement. Much of the 'dance' material of these videodances comprises pedestrian movement rather than dance steps, or even no human movement at all, as in *Birds* (2000) by David Hinton.

> The more choreographic thinking there is in a film the more successful any film is likely to be. The more the film director is communicating through action rather than through dialogue for instance, the more successful his film will be. The more he's thinking about the relationship between a person and a space, about rhythmic relationships between actions, then the more he's using the medium of film effectively.
>
> (Hinton in Williams, 1999)

This videodance and many other examples are available to view on youtube and also on many dance company websites as promotion movies. YouTube makes the screening of short film more accessible than ever before. Technology is now relatively simple, affordable and understandable, and anybody can start exploring with video. YouTube, mobile phones, i-pods and all kinds of equipment can be used to experiment artistically. Some video clips are already influenced by animation and game design, and surely some new developments will take place when these genres start collaborating. Imagine dance in a virtual environment with 3D animation – dancers dancing with us in our studios or in our living rooms.

As first year Dance Studies students, you might start by making mini-video clips on your mobile phone, or working with a small group of people with one video camera: conceptualizing your ideas, creating a story-board, exploring new spaces or dancing with your virtual partner on the screen behind you. A first study unit might explore relationships between the body, choreography and technology through basic techniques for shooting and editing material; a study of live and recorded dance works, their histories and development; explorations with fixed and moving cameras, designing space, shifts of perspective; and explorations of the moving body, and projections in performance. At this stage, the emphasis is on exploration and creativity; perhaps you might devise a small group choreography with fellow students, film it, edit it and put it on YouTube, as our first year Dance Studies students at the University of Malta are encouraged to do.

Indeed, this chapter has attempted to introduce intending students, their parents and careers teachers to some of the applications of Dance Studies in terms of social dance, dance in education, community dance, and dance and technology. Together with the specific areas of study in the last five chapters, these are all sub-disciplines of Dance Studies, and thus can be considered as possible applications for your future career. In the conclusion which follows, we will discuss how important it is for you to do some research about the Dance degrees that you are interested in before you make your final choice. Who knows, for example, if a growing curiosity about dance and technology might determine the journey of your future career?

CONCLUSION: YOUR FIRST STEPS TOWARDS STUDYING DANCE

It may be simplistic to warn the reader that, though an increasing number of Dance programmes are on offer in higher education in many countries of the world, they do not each offer the same areas of study. Indeed, one of the delights of researching the various courses available to intending students – whether straight from secondary education or entering as mature students – is to discover *what* is on offer and where. There are literally thousands of Dance programmes worldwide to choose from, with many national, cultural and discipline-specific differences. If, after having read this book, you are still enthusiastic about embarking on this adventure, then please make sure that you research all your options carefully. Your career in dance may never make you wealthy, but it has been an extremely creative, satisfying and stimulating journey for most of the students, dancers, choreographers, lecturers and dance practitioners with whom I have had the pleasure of working.

Do not imagine that the study of dance in the university sector is necessarily the route to a performance career with a major company. Dancers in major ballet companies, for example, are far more likely to have been educated in a ballet school which is established and directly related to a specific company. Students who are lucky enough to gain a place at a performing arts conservatory/conservatoire will be in the minority; as an example, only 5.5 per cent of applicants achieved a place at the Juilliard School in New York in 2011. Indeed, only a very small percentage of graduates will make successful, full-time careers as performers, though a relatively large proportion will be sufficiently multi-skilled to be able to maintain a balance of dancing, teaching and choreographing, with all of the personal administration that is normally involved.

Dance is not a soft subject; it requires physical, emotional and intellectual stamina to study dance effectively at the university level, and it is important that each potential participant has considered his or her choice from every perspective. Today, university websites are a mine of information, offering course descriptions, glossy photographs, marketing material and staff research profiles. But what is it that they do not tell you? Are the entry requirements made clear? Will you have an opportunity to audition, have an interview with someone from the department and ask all your well-prepared questions? Can you view all the resources – dance studios, theatre, library, computer suites, classrooms and student accommodation? What are the other programmes in the faculty, and to what extent do they collaborate and influence each other? To what extent does the course provide a generalist or liberal arts spectrum, and is it possible to specialize?

And like many other young people who go to university each year, what do you imagine it would be like to live away from home? Do you prefer an urban city environment or a leafy suburb, countryside or town? Many students live in halls of residence at least for the first year of their academic courses, or longer. Others move out into shared housing as soon as possible. Cities may provide more social opportunities – theatres, clubs, galleries – but may also be larger, more expensive and less friendly than an institution based in a smaller town.

You might enjoy dancing for pleasure – indeed, that is probably one of the reasons for reading this book – but dancing and studying every day throughout a degree programme can be exhausting and stimulating in equal measure. Try to be pragmatic and also realistic about your potential as a student; consider your personal areas of interest and what you might want to achieve. There may be injuries, however carefully you train and practise; there will be deadlines and other pressures to perform in shows and assessments, to complete essays and term papers, to choreograph new works, to present lecture-demonstrations, to teach creative workshops or sit for examinations. In addition, a degree in Dance Studies cannot normally be achieved without working closely with friends, peers and colleagues in collaborative situations, participating in shared decision-making, as in the other disciplines in the performing arts. You cannot go through life as a soloist.

One of the issues often raised by parents and teachers is to do with potential career opportunities and the need to earn a living. The first reminder is that not everyone will join a company and tour the world. And even if you do, there will come a time when touring and performing lose their charm, and you want to redirect your energies into dance teaching and lecturing, directing, writing, dance administration, workshop leading and the like. Some may go on to study at postgraduate level, specializing at Master's level, MFA or PhD; others will take on responsibility for directing a dance company, running a school, making a dance film or choreographing for television. Others may decide to go on to study dance movement therapy and use movement and dance to facilitate emotional, physical, social, mental and spiritual growth.

If, after all these warnings, I have not put you off your ambition, and you still want to commit to higher education in Dance, then I have no doubt that you will succeed. You will have an intense experience, develop your intellect, make good friends, see yourself progress and your body become an expressive instrument. Try to stay open-minded and flexible, even when confronted with new ideas, or attitudes that are radically different from those that you were introduced to when you first started dancing. The discipline of dance is a growth area and the potential for talented and imaginative graduates is enormous.

GLOSSARY

Abstractionism   Using and working only with parts of an overall concept or movement phrase.

Aesthetic   Specific appearance, effect or style.

Alignment   Consideration of the skeletal structure in the dancer's posture.

Amateur dance   Dancing as a pastime rather than as a profession.

Appreciation (dance)   Understanding the whole construction of steps, phrases, sections, the nexus of patterns, repeated movements, variation and canon in relation to the relationships of the dancers; the progression and the high points or climaxes of the dance.

Barre   A stationary handrail that is used during ballet warm-up exercises. The term also refers to the exercises that are performed at the barre, as well as that part of a ballet class that incorporates barre exercises.

Choreography   The art of creating dances.

Classical dance   A classical dance form characterized by grace and precision of movement and by elaborate formal gestures, steps and poses.

Classicism   Aesthetic attitudes and principles based on the culture, art and literature of ancient Greece and Rome, and characterized by emphasis on form, simplicity, proportion and restrained emotion.

Clog dancing   A type of folk dance with roots in traditional European dancing, early African American dance, and traditional Cherokee dance in which the dancer's footwear is used musically by striking the heel, the toe, or both in unison against a floor or each other to create audible percussive rhythms.

Codified techniques Formal, pre-established dance techniques.

Collaborator (choreographer) Interactive method of choreography between two or more collaborators.

Community dance A field promoting dance practices with groups and communities to express diverse local identities and to raise awareness about social, political and environmental issues.

Composition (dance) Learning the skills, devices and approaches to making dances.

Contemporary dance A style and philosophy of dance developed during the twentieth century, following modern dance developments in the USA.

Diaspora The movement or migration of displaced people away from an established homeland; a community of those who maintain strong cultural ties with their homeland.

Didactic (choreographer) Instructional method of choreography.

Embody Represent in bodily form.

Enchaînements Long complex movement phrases.

Facilitator (choreographer) Nurturing and mentoring choreographic method.

Female A matter of biology.

Feminine A set of culturally defined characteristics.

Feminist A political position.

Flexibility Capable of being bent or flexed.

Folklore The traditional beliefs, myths, tales and practices of a people, transmitted orally.

Freestyle dancing Can be defined as any style of dance where the moves are not thought out ahead and where no choreography of the moves occurs before the dance begins.

Gender studies An interdisciplinary study which analyses race, ethnicity, sexuality and location. In Gender Studies, the term 'gender' is used to refer to the social and cultural constructions of masculinities and femininities, not to the state of being male or female.

Genre A category of artistic composition.

Group dynamic Processes which develop through interaction among members of a given group and could include norms, roles, relations, development, need to belong, social influence and effects on behaviour.

Historical dancing A collective term covering a wide variety of dance types from the past as they are danced in the present.

Hybrid Of mixed origin or composition.

Interdisciplinary The merging or synthesis of two or more academic disciplines or styles normally considered distinct.

Isolation Movement made by one body part, separate from other parts of the body.

Kinaesthetics The sense by which motion, weight and the position of various body parts is perceived.

Kinesiology The study of the anatomy, physiology and mechanics of body movement, especially in humans.

Kinetic energy The capacity for work or vigorous activity; vigour; power.

Modern dance A serious theatrical dance developed in the USA in the 1930s, outside the classical ballet tradition.

Morris dancing A form of English folk dance usually accompanied by music. It is based on rhythmic stepping and the execution of choreographed figures by a group of dancers.

Motifs Short movement phrases capable of being developed.

Natya shastra An ancient Indian treatise on the performing arts, encompassing theatre, dance and music.

Representational dance vocabulary Movements that show a relationship between world/art and copy/model.

Romanticism An international artistic and philosophical movement that redefined the fundamental ways in which people in Western cultures thought about themselves and about their world.

Rote learning A learning technique which focuses on memorization.

Site-specific work Work that is created for a specific site or place.

Social dancing Social dance is a major category or classification of dance forms or dance styles, where sociability and socializing are the primary focuses of the dancing. Social dances can be danced with a variety of partners and still be led and followed in a relaxed, easy atmosphere.

Solar plexus Complex of radiating nerves at the pit of the stomach.

Somatic Of the body (Greek), corporeal, physical, sensate.

Sprung floor A shock-absorbent floor that protects dancers' bodies.

Stamina Endurance or strength.

Street dancing An umbrella term used to describe dance styles that evolved outside dance studios in any available open space such as streets, parks, school yards or nightclubs.

Tanztheater A performance form that combines dance, speaking, singing and chanting, conventional theatre and the use of props, set, and costumes in one amalgam. It is performed by trained dancers. Usually there is no narrative plot; instead, specific situations, fears, and human conflicts are presented.

Time-signature A sign that indicates the metre of a piece of music e.g. 2/4, 5/8.

Turn out (movement) Outward rotation of the hips and feet.

Versatility Adaptivity, having multiple capabilities.

Videodance Genre of film making specific to dance and choreography, using stylized or pedestrian movements, though protagonists could be human, animal or inanimate objects, using visual rhythm and perhaps special effects. Other terminology could include: dancefilm, choreography for the camera, cinedance, and dance for the camera.

REFERENCES

PRINTED SOURCES

Abbs, Peter (1989) *A is for Aesthetic: Essays on Creative and Aesthetic Education* London: Falmer Press

Adair, Christy (1992) *Women and Dance: Sylphs and Sirens* Basingstoke: Macmillan

Adshead, Janet (1981) *The Study of Dance* London: Dance Books

Adshead, Janet (ed.) (1988) *Dance Analysis: Theory and Practice* London: Dance Books

Amans, Diane (ed.) (2008) *An Introduction to Community Dance Practice* Basingstoke: Palgrave Macmillan

Appleyard, Brian (1984) *The Culture Club: Crisis in the Arts* London: Faber and Faber

Argyle, Michael (1972) *Bodily Communication* London: Methuen

Arts Council (1983) *The Arts Council and Education: A Policy Statement* London: Arts Council of Great Britain

Ashley, Linda (2008) *Essential Guide to Dance* third edition, London: Hodder Education

Ashton, Frederick (1984) 'Sir Frederick Ashton in Conversation with Alastair Macaulay, *Dance Theatre Journal* 2.3, pp. 2–7

Au, Susan (1988) *Ballet and Modern Dance* London: Thames and Hudson

Auslander, P. (1999) *Liveness: Performance in a Mediatized Culture* London: Routledge

Banes, Sally (1983) *Democracy's Body: Judson Dance Theater* 1962–64 Epping: Bowker

Banes, Sally (1984) 'A History of Post-Modern Dance from the 1960's to the 1980's', Lecture to the NYU Gallatin Division students on the postgraduate interdisciplinary seminar module, 22 March.

Banes, Sally (1987) *Terpsichore in Sneakers* second edition, Middletown, Conn.: Wesleyan University Press

Banes, Sally (1994) *Writing Dancing in the Age of Postmodernism* Hanover, Pa., and London: Wesleyan University Press

Bannerman, Christopher (2000) Personal Interview, 11 November, London

Barry, Peter (1995) *Beginning Theory: An Introduction to Literary and Cultural Theory* Manchester: Manchester University Press

Bartenieff, Irmgard and Dori Lewis (1980) *Body Movement: Coping with the Environment* London and New York: Routledge

Bell, Clive (1914) *Art* London: Chatto and Windus

Birringer, J. (1998) *Media and Performance: Along the Border* Baltimore, Ma., and London: John Hopkins University Press

Birringer, J. (2000) *Performance on the Edge: Transformations of Culture* London: Continuum

Blom, L.A. and Chaplin L.T. (1982) *The Intimate Act of Choreography* Pittsburgh, Pa.: University of Pittsburgh Press

Blom, L.A. and Chaplin L.T. (1988) *The Moment of Movement: Dance Improvisation* London: Dance Books

Bloomfield, Anne (1989) 'The Philosophical and Artistic Tradition of Dance in British Education', in *Young People Dancing: An International Perspective* vol. 1, London: DaCi/Roehampton Institute pp. 10–20

Bradley, Karen K. (2009) *Rudolf Laban* Abingdon and New York: Routledge

Bremser, M. (ed.) (1999) *Fifty Contemporary Choreographers* London and New York: Routledge

Brinson, Peter (1982) 'The Nature of Collaboration', *Dance as Education* ACGB/DES

Brinson, Peter (1991) *Dance as Education: Towards a National Dance Culture* London: Falmer Press

Broadhurst, S. and Machon (2007) *Performance and Technology: Practices of Virtual Embodiment and Interactivity* New York: Palgrave

Burt, Ramsay (1985) Interview with Ramsay Burt, *New Dance* 35 (January) p. 10

Burt, Ramsay (1998) *Alien Bodies: Representations of Modernity, Race and Nation in Early Modern Dance* London: Routledge

Burt, Ramsay (2006) *Judson Dance Theatre: Performative Traces* London and New York: Routledge

Burt, Ramsay (2007) *The Male Dancer: Bodies, Spectacle, Sexualities*, second edition, London: Routledge

Burt, Ramsay (2010) 'Nijinsky: Modernism and Heterodox Representations of Masculinity', in Alexandra Carter and Janet O'Shea (eds) *The Routledge Dance Studies Reader* London and New York: Routledge, pp. 220–228

Butterworth, Jo (2004) 'Teaching Choreography in HE: A Process Continuum Model', *Research in Dance Education* 5.1, pp. 45–67.

Butterworth, Jo (2009) 'Too Many Cooks? A framework for Dance Making and Devising', in Jo Butterworth and Liesbeth Wildschut (eds) *Contemporary*

Choreography: A Critical Reader London and New York: Routledge, pp. 177–194

Butterworth, Jo and Gill Clarke (1998) *Dance Makers Portfolio: Conversations with Choreographers* Wakefield: Centre for Dance and Theatre Studies at Bretton Hall

Butterworth, Jo and Liesbeth Wildschut (2009) *Contemporary Choreography: A Critical Reader* London and New York: Routledge

Calais-Germain, Blandine (2007) *Anatomy of Movement* Seattle: Eastland Press

Campbell, Patrick (ed.) (1996) *Analysing Performance: A Critical Reader* Manchester and New York: Manchester University Press

Carter, Alexandra (ed.) (1997) *The Routledge Dance Studies Reader* London and New York: Routledge

Carter, Alexandra (ed.) (2004) *Rethinking Dance History: A Reader* London and New York: Routledge

Carter, Alexandra and Janet O'Shea (2010) *The Routledge Dance Studies Reader* second edition, London and New York: Routledge

Caspersen, Dana (2000) 'It Starts from Any Point: Bill and the Frankfurt Ballet', *Choreography and Dance* 5.3, pp. 25–26

Celichowska, Renata (2000) *The Erick Hawkins Modern Dance Technique* Princeton, NJ: Dance Horizons

Chang, Jeff (2005) *Can't Stop Won't Stop: A History of the Hip-Hop Generation* London: Ebury Press

Chapple, F. and C. Kattenbelt (eds) (2006) *Intermediality in Theatre and Performance* Amsterdam and New York: IFTH

Chazin-Bennahum, Judith (2005) *Teaching Dance Studies: A University Primer* New York: Routledge

Claid, Emilyn (2006) *Yes? No! Maybe: Seductive Ambiguities in Dance* London and New York: Routledge

Clarke, Mary and Clement Crisp (1989) *London Contemporary Dance Theatre: The First 21 Years* London: Dance Books

Clinton, Lola (1993) *Community Development and the Arts* London: CDF Publications

Cohan, Robert (1967) 'Robert Cohan Talks to Dance and Dancers on Contemporary Dance in Britain', *Dance and Dancers* (September), p. 19

Cohen, Selma Jeanne (1974) *Dance as a Theatre Art: Source Readings in Dance History from 1581 to the Present* New York: Dodd, Mead

Cohen, Selma Jeanne (1992) *Dance as a Theatre Art: Source Readings in Dance History from 1581 to the Present* Princeton, NJ: Princeton Book Company

Collingwood, R. (1938) *The Principles of Art* Oxford: Clarendon Press

Copeland, Roger and Marshall Cohen (eds) (1983) *What is Dance? Readings in Theory and Criticism* Oxford: Oxford University Press

Coton, A.V. (1975) *Writings on Dance 1938–1968*, selected and ed. Kathrine Sorley Walker and Lillian Hadakin, London: Dance Books

Counsell, Colin and Laurie Wolf (eds) (2001) *Performance Analysis: An Introductory Course Book*, London and New York: Routledge

Croce, Benedetto (1922) *Aesthetic: As Science of Expression and General Linguistic*, translated by Douglas Ainslie New York: Noonday Press

Cunningham, Merce (1985, 2000) *The Dancer and the Dance* London: Marion Boyars

Dearden, R.F. (1965) 'Instruction and Learning by Discovery', in R.S. Peters (ed.) *The Concept of Education* London: Routledge and Kegan Paul, pp. 135–155

De Beauvoir, Simone ([1949] 1989) *The Second Sex* Harmondsworth: Penguin

Delamater, Jerome (1981) *Dance in the Hollywood Musical* Ann Arbor, Mich.: UMI Research Press

Desmond, Jane (1999) 'Engendering Dance: Feminist Enquiry and Dance Research', in Sondra Horton Fraleigh and Penelope Hanstein (eds) *Researching Dance: Evolving Modes of Enquiry* London: Dance Books pp. 309–333

Dewey, John (1934) *Art as Experience* New York: Mitton, Balch

Dewey, John (1958) *Experience and Nature* New York: Dover

Diamond, Elin (1996) *Performance and Cultural Politics*, London: Routledge

Dietz, Ulrich (2010) 'Mind and Body: An Interview with Wayne McGregor', FAR Programme, Sadler's Wells, 17–20 November 2010

Dils, A. and Albright, A.C. (eds) (2001) *Moving History/Dancing Cultures: A Dance History Reader* Middletown, Conn.: Wesleyan University Press

Drummond, John (1996) 'A Golden Stage', *Dance Theatre Journal* 13.2 (Autumn/Winter), pp. 10–12

Early, Fergus (1987) 'Liberation Notes, etc. A paper from the Chisenhale/NODM Weekend to celebrate New Dance, May 1986', *New Dance* 40, pp. 10–12

FAR Programme (2010) 'Random Dance at Sadlers Wells Theatre', London

Farjeon, Annabel (2010) 'Choreographers: Dancing for de Valois and Ashton', in Alexandra Carter and Janet O'Shea (eds) *The Routledge Dance Studies Reader* London and New York: Routledge pp. 23–28

Fisher, Jennifer and Antony Shay (2009) *When Men Dance: Choreographing Masculinities* New York: Oxford University Press

Forman, Murray, and Mark Anthony Neal (2004) *That's the Joint: The Hip-Hop Studies Reader* New York and Abingdon: Routledge

Foster, Susan L. (1986) *Reading Dancing: Bodies and Subjects in Contemporary American Dance* Berkeley and Los Angeles: University of California Press

Franklin, Eric (2004) *Conditioning for Dance: Training for Peak Performance in All Dance Forms* Champaign, Ill.: Human Kinetics

Fry, Roger (1926) *Transformations: Critical and Speculative Essays on Art* London: Chatto and Windus

Geertz, Clifford (1973) *The Interpretation of Cultures: Selected Essays*, New York: Basic Books

Graham, Martha (1991) *Blood Memory: An Autobiography* New York: Doubleday

Grau, Andrée and Stephanie Jordan (2000) *Europe Dancing: Perspectives on Theatre Dance and Cultural Identity* London and New York: Routledge

Hall, Stuart (1977) 'Culture, Media and the "Ideological Effect"', in J. Curran, M. Gurevitch and J. Woollacott (eds) *Mass Communication and Society* London: Arnold/Open University Press, pp. 315–348

Hanna, Judith Lynne (1979) *To Dance Is Human: A Theory of Non-verbal Communication* Austin: University of Texas Press

Hanna, Thomas (1988) *Somatics: Reawakening the Mind's Control of Movement, Flexibility and Health* Cambridge, Mass.: Da Capo

Harrison-Barbet, Anthony (2001) *Mastering Philosophy* Basingstoke: Macmillan

Hawkins, Alma (1991) *Moving from Within: A New Method for Dance Making* Pennington, NJ: a cappella

Hayes, Claire (1978) 'Many Ways of Seeing – Dance at the Riverside Studios', *New Dance* 6 (Spring), p. 6

Hodgens, Pauline (1975) 'The Choreographic Structure of Robert Cohan's Stabat Mater', in Janet Adshead (ed.) *Choreography, Principles and Practice* Guildford: National Resource Centre for Dance, pp. 245–255

Hodgson, John (2001) *Mastering Movement: The Life and Work of Rudolf Laban* London: Methuen

Hodgson, John and Valerie Preston-Dunlop (1992) *Rudolf Laban: An Introduction to his Work and Influence* Plymouth: Northcote House

Howard, Robin (1966) 'Transatlantic Influence', *Dance and Dancers* (October), pp. 28–31

Humphrey, Doris ([1959] 1999) *The Art of Making Dances* second edition, London: Dance Books

Jakobson, R. (1972) 'Linguistics and Poetics', in R. De George and E. De George (eds) *The Structuralists: From Marx to Levi-Strauss* New York: Anchor Books

Jasper, Linda (1995) 'Tensions in the Definition of Community Dance', in Janet Adshead-Lansdale (ed.) *Border Tensions: Dance and Discourse* Guildford: University of Surrey, p. 181

Jordan, Stephanie (1992) *Striding Out: Aspects of Contemporary and New Dance in Britain* London: Dance Books

Jordan, S. and A. Grau (1996) *Following Sir Fred's Steps: Ashton's Legacy* London Dance Books

Jordan, Stephanie and Helen Thomas ([1998] 2010) 'Dance and Gender: Formalism and semiotics reconsidered' *The Routledge Dance Studies Reader* London and New York: Routledge pp. 149–157

Kaye, Nick (1994) *Postmodernism and Performance* Basingstoke: Macmillan

Kelly, Owen (1984) *Community, Art and the State: Storming the Citadels* London: Commedia

Kershaw, Baz (1992) *The Politics of Performance* London and New York: Routledge

Khoo, Mavin (2011) Personal Interview, 21 January, University of Malta

Kostelanetz, Richard (ed.) (1992) *Merce Cunningham: Dancing in Space and Time* London: Dance Books

Laban, Rudolf (1948) *Modern Educational Dance* London: MacDonald and Evans

Laban, Rudolf (1971) *Mastery of Movement*, third edition revised by Lisa Ullmann London: MacDonald and Evans

Laban, Rudolf (1975) *Ein Leben für den Tanz* (Dresden: Carl Reisser, 1935) translated and edited by Lisa Ullmann as *A Life for Dance* London: MacDonald and Evans

Langer, Susanne (1953) *Feeling and Form* London: Routledge and Kegan Paul

Lawton, Denis (1973) *Social Change, Educational Theory and Curriculum Planning* London: Hodder and Stoughton

Leebolt, Martha (2011) Personal Interview (email), 9 March

Lewis, Daniel (1999) *The Illustrated Dance Technique of José Limón* Princeton, NJ: Princeton Book Company Publishers

Liggitt, Rachel (1991) 'The Dancer as Creator: Movement Exploration with Groups of Adults with Learning Difficulties' (unpublished essay submitted as part of Practical Project Assignment, December)

Livet, Anne (ed) (1978) *Contemporary Dance* New York: Abberville Press

Macauley, Alistair (1984) 'Sir Frederick Ashton in Conversation with Alastair Macaulay', *Dance Theatre Journal* 2.3 (Autumn), pp. 2–7

McCaw, Dick (ed.) (2011) *The Laban Sourcebook* London and New York: Routledge

McDonagh, Don (1973) *The Rise and Fall and Rise of Modern Dance* London: Dance Books

McDonagh, Don (1983) *George Balanchine* Boston, Mass: Twayne

MacDonald, Barry (2000) 'How Education Became Nobody's Business', in Herbert Altricher and John Elliott (eds) *Images of Educational Change* Buckingham: Open University Press, pp. 20–36

Mackrell, Judith (1997) *Reading Dance* London: Michael Joseph

Mackrell, Judith (1984) 'Umbrella 1983: Some Thoughts and Reviews', *Dance Theatre Journal* 2.1 (Spring), p. 30

Mackrell, Judith (1992) *Out of Line: The Story of British New Dance* London: Dance Books

Madden, Dorothy (1996) *You Call Me Louis, not Mr Horst,* Amsterdam: Harwood Academic Publishers

Manning, Susan Allene and Melissa Benson (2001) 'Interrupted Continuities: Modern Dance in Germany' in Ann Dils and Ann Cooper Albright (eds) *Moving History/Dancing Cultures: a dance history reader* Hanover, PA: Wesleyan University Press pp. 218–227

Matarasso, Francois (1994) *Regular Marvels: A Handbook for Animateurs, Practitioners and Development Workers in Dance, Mime Music and Literature* Leicester: CDMF

May, Rollo (1975) *The Courage to Create* New York and London: W.W. Norton

Midgelow, Vidal (ed.) (2007) *Reworking the Ballet: Counter-narratives and Alternative Bodies* Abingdon and New York: Routledge

Midgette, Anne (2000) 'Forsythe in Frankfurt: A Documentation in Three Movements', *Choreography and Dance* 5.3, pp. 13–23

Minton, S.C. (1986, 1997) *Choreography: A Basic Approach Using Improvisation* Champaign, Ill.: Human Kinetics

Newson, Lloyd (2009) Interview on Pina Bausch, *Guardian* 3 July

Nii-Yartey, Francis (2009) 'Principles of African Choreography: Some Perspectives from Ghana', in Jo Butterworth and Liesbeth Wildschut (eds) *Contemporary Choreography: A Critical Reader* London and New York: Routledge pp. 254–268

North, Marion (1971) *An Introduction to Movement Study and Teaching* London: MacDonald and Evans

O'Shea, Janet (2007) *At Home in the World* Middletown, Conn.: Wesleyan University Press

Pateman, Trevor (1991) *Key Concepts: A Guide to Aesthetics, Criticism and the Arts in Education* London: Falmer Press

Pavis, Patrice (2003) *Analysing Performance: Theater, Dance and Film* Ann Arbor: University of Michigan Press

Percival, John (1971) *Experimental Dance* London: Studio Vista

Percival, John (1980) *Modern Ballet* rev. edition, London: The Herbert Press

Preston, H. (2006) 'Choreography the Frame: A Critical Investigation into how Dance for the Camera Extends the Conceptual and Artistic Boundaries of Dance', *Research in Dance Education* 7.1, pp. 75–87

Preston, Valerie (1963) *A Handbook for Modern Educational Dance* London: MacDonald and Evans

Preston-Dunlop, V. (1998) *Looking at Dances: A Choreological Perspective on Choreography* London: Verve

Preston-Dunlop, Valerie (1998, 2008) *Rudolf Laban: An Extraordinary Life* London: Dance Books

Preston-Dunlop, Valerie and Ana Sanchez-Colberg (2002) *Dance and the Performative* London: Verve

Read, Herbert ([1931] 1949) *The Meaning of Art* London: Penguin

Redfern, Betty (1983) *Dance, Art and Aesthetics* London: Dance Books

Redfern, H.B. (1973) *Concepts in Modern Educational Dance* London: Henry Kimpton

Sanders, Lorna (2004) *Henri Oguike's Front Line: Creative Insights* Alton, Hants: Dance Books

Schön, Donald (1987) *Educating the Reflective Practitioner* San Francisco: Jossey-Bass

Sheppard, Anne (1987) *Aesthetics: An Introduction to the Philosophy of Art* Oxford: Oxford University Press

Smith-Autard, J. (2010) *Dance Composition* sixth edition, London: Methuen Drama

Smith-Autard, Jacqueline (1994, 2002) *The Art of Dance in Education* London: A. & C. Black

South Bank Show (1993) 'Sylvie Guillem', ITV South Bank, 30 October

Stern, Carrie (2007) 'Erick Hawkins', in *Dance Teacher* (September), www. dance-teacher.com/context/erick-hawkins

Stevens, Sarah (1989) 'Dance Teacher Education in Britain in the 1990s', in *Young People Dancing* vol. 1, London: DaCi/Roehampton Institute, pp. 288–296

Stodelle, Ernestine (1979) *The Dance Technique of Doris Humphrey and Its Creative Potential* Princeton, NJ: Princeton Books

Stolnitz, Jerome (1960) 'The Aesthetic Attitude', *Aesthetics and the Philosophy of Art Criticism: A Critical Introduction* pp. 32–42, reprinted in Hospers, J. (1969) *Introductory Readings in Aesthetics* London: Collier Macmillan

Thomson, Christopher (1988) 'Community Dance: What Community ... What Dance?', in *Young People Dancing: An International Perspective* vol. 3 London: DaCi, pp. 88–98

Todd, Mabel Elsworth (1937) *The Thinking Body: Study of the Dynamic Forces of Dynamic Man* Princeton, NJ: Princeton University Press

Tomkins, Calvin (1968) *The Bride and the Bachelor: Five Masters of the Avant-Garde* London: Penguin Books

Turnbull, Audrey (1969) 'Teachers and Teaching: the London School of Contemporary Dance', *Dance and Dancers* 20.8 (September), p. 50

Turner, Margery (1971) *New Dance: Approaches to Non-Literal Choreography* Pittsburgh, Pa.: University of Pittsburgh Press

Vaughan, David (1996) 'Ashton Now', in Stephanie Jordan and Andrée Grau (eds), *Following Sir Fred's Steps: Ashton's Legacy* London: Dance Books pp. 1–2

Whitley, Ann (2000) Personal Interview, 18 April, Clapham, North Yorkshire

Wigman, Mary (1984) *The Mary Wigman Book: Her writings* ed and trans. by Walter Sorell Middletown, Conn.: Wesleyan University Press

Williams, C. (2002) 'Beyond Criticism: Lerman's "Critical Response Process" in the Dance Composition Classroom', *Journal of Dance Education* 2.3, pp. 93–99

Williams, Peter (1969) 'Sturdy Foreign Roots', *Dance and Dancers* (November), p. 24

Wilson, F.M.G. (1997) *In Just Order Move: The Progress of the Laban Centre for Movement and Dance 1946–1996* London and New Jersey: Athlone Press

Wolff, Janet (1981) *The Social Production of Art* London: Macmillan

WEBSITES

http://education.kosmix.com/topic/Beijing_Dance_Academy#ixzz1Ed2DpRYG (accessed 20 Feb 2011)

http://butoh.net (accessed 5 Mar 2011)

http://genderandsexuality.as.nyu.edu/page/home (accessed 28 Feb 2011)

http://kennethmacmillan.com/ballets/all-works/1970–1977/manon.html (accessed 6 Mar 2011)

http://northernballet.com/confidential/review.php (accessed 1 Mar 2011)

http://noyam.org/index.php?id=1 (accessed 22 Jan 2011)

http://synchronousobjects.osu.edu/content.html (accessed 21 Jan 2011))

www.archive.org/details/tolstoyonart00tolsuoft (accessed 22 Feb 2011)

www.armitagegonedance.org/karole-armitage/artists-statement (accessed 1 Mar 2011)

www.ausdance.org.au (accessed 11 Feb 2011)

www.ballet.co.uk/magazines/yr_02/…interview_deborah_bull.htm (accessed 12 Feb 2011)

www.communitydance.org.uk (accessed 21 Dec 2011)

www.complicite.org (accessed 8 Mar 2011)

www.cullbergbaletten.se/EN/Home (accessed 10 Mar 2011)

www.danceexchange.org (accessed 11 Feb 2011)

www.danceuk.org (accessed 21 Dec 2011)

www.danz.org.nz (accessed 11 Feb 2011)

www.dv8.co.uk (accessed 11 Jan 2011)

www.efvalilia.se (accessed 21 Feb 2011)

Erick Hawkins Dance: www.erickhawkinsdance.org (accessed 3 May 2011)

www.franticassembly.co.uk (accessed 8 Mar 2011)

www.grotest-maru.de (accessed 8 Mar 2011)

www.hkapa.edu/asp/dance/dance_introduction.asp (accessed 8 Dec 2010

www.houstonballet.org (accessed 2 Mar 2011)

www.kalakshetra.net (accessed 20 Feb 2011)

www.kennethmacmillan.com (accessed 1 Mar 2011)

www.laballet.com/classes/contdanceprog/index.html (accessed 13 Dec 2010)

www.limon.org (accessed 20 Feb 2011)

www.Marianrose.com (accessed 11 Feb 2011)

www.merce.org (accessed 19 Jan 2011)

www.michaelclarkcompany.com/ (accessed 1 Mar 2011)

www.national.ballet.ca (accessed 2 Mar 2011)

www.ndeo.org (accessed 8 Mar 2011)

www.ndt.nl

www.newstatesman.com/dance/2010/11/trisha-brown-different-piece (accessed 14 May 2011)

www.nikolaislouis.org (accessed 12 Feb 2011

www.northernballet.com

www.nutritionaustralia.org

www.Nutrition.gov

www.nutrition.org.uk

www.nycballet.com/company/viewing.html (accessed 22 Feb 2011)

www.pbs.org/wnet/americanmasters/episodes/alwin-nikolais/about-alwin-nikolais/674/ (accessed 28 Jan 2011)

www.rambert.org.uk

www.roh.org.uk

www.roh.org.uk/discover/ballet/index.aspx (accessed 3 Mar 2011)

www.sadlerswells.com (accessed 19 Feb 2011)

www.sadlerswellsisdance.com/#/category/takingpart (accessed 23 Feb 2011)

www.siobhandaviesreplay.com (accessed 21 Nov 2010)

www.somaticsed.com (accessed 5 Mar 2011)

www.scottisharts.org.uk/1/artsinscotland/dance/features/archive/stylecon-temporarydance.aspx (accessed 10 Dec 2010)

www.sussex.ac.uk/gender (accessed 28 Feb 2011)

www.telegraph.co.uk/culture/culturecritics/sarahcrompton/3563262/Wayne-McGregors-Infra-sumptuous-beauty-and-shimmering-possibility.html (accessed 11 Mar 2011)

www.telegraph.co.uk/culture/theatre/dance/8351914/cleopatra_Northern-Ballet_(eds-Grand-Theatre-review.html (accessed 6 Mar 2011)

www.thestage.co.uk/reviews/review.php/3i426/cleopatra (accessed 6 Mar 2011)

www.youtube.com

INDEX

Page numbers in *italics* denote tables, those in **bold** denote figures.